Introduction to Law and the Legal System

Fifth Edition

Study Guide

Introduction to Law and the Legal System

Fifth Edition

Study Guide

Grilliot/Schubert

Elisabeth J. Medvedow, Esq.

Houghton Mifflin Company   Boston   Toronto
Dallas   Geneva, Illinois   Palo Alto   Princeton, New Jersey

Sponsoring Editor: Denise Clinton
Development Editor: Julie Hogenboom
Ancillary Coordinator: Elena Di Cesare
Manufacturing Coordinator: Sharon Pearson
Marketing Manager: Michael Ginley

Printed in the U.S.A.

Library of Congress Catalog Card Number: 91-71990

ISBN: 0-395-59229-1

BCDEFGHIJ-B-99876543

Contents

Preface

The purpose of this study guide to the fifth edition of *Introduction to Law and the Legal System* is to help you learn the basic principles presented in the text. The study guide is not a substitute for careful studying of the text or for attending classes. It can help you, however, by identifying important concepts and terms and by asking you questions about them.

Here are a few suggestions for studying this material:

1. Get your hands on a legal dictionary and use it often. Several good paperback editions are available in bookstores. The language of law will be foreign to most of you and until you become familiar with the terminology, you will find the going difficult. It really is essential that you learn the meaning of these strange words and terms. If you start right out looking everything up that you don't understand, you will gradually develop your vocabulary and your ability to follow what is being said in the text.

2. Use your textbook properly. *Be an active rather than a passive reader.* This means that you should follow a few steps that are designed to help you read more effectively. Begin by **previewing** the assigned reading in the test: quickly skim over the major topics that are addressed in the chapter so that you have a basic idea of what you are about to read. What is it that ties this material together? How does this reading seem to relate to what you have previously read? Next, **read** the assigned material carefully. Take good notes of the important points and new vocabulary that are addressed in the text. Understanding the facts of a case is necessary, but remember that every case has been selected because it illustrates one or more important principles that relate to the receding textual discussion. The last step involves **summarizing** these principles.

Summarizing means that you should briefly list the general points that you have identified as being most important in each case. After you have previewed, read, and summarized the material, try to answer the case questions at the end of each case. When you finish an entire chapter, read the chapter questions.

3. Turn to the study guide after you have read a chapter in the text book. Read the chapter overview. It sums up the most important points in the chapter. Read over the list of key topics that follow it. Are there any terms that cause you to hesitate or feel insecure? If so, look them up and put the answers in your notes.

4. Finally, test yourself by answering the review questions at the end of each chapter in the study guide. They are designed to give you an indication of how much you remember about the material. There are four kinds: questions on key terms, true-false questions, multiple-choice questions, and completion questions. The answers to all study guide questions are given in the back of the study guide. Do not look back at the answers until you have finished trying to answer a given set of review questions. Do not be rattled if you missed a good many of them. Just go back and review the area of the chapter that discusses those particular points.

These four steps should help you prepare for class discussions as well as to study for examinations. My experience in studying and teaching this subject for many years has taught me that few people are able to use the cramming method of studying for examinations successfully. You should study the text and the study guide regularly if you expect to learn the material. One good way to determine if you are ready to be tested on the material is for you to either verbally explain each topic to a friend or classmate or write yourself a short essay. If you find that you can put what you "know" into words you will probably be able to explain yourself to the satisfaction of your instructor.

I hope that through this study guide, you will increase your understanding of legal terminology, reasoning, procedures, and theory. This legal foundation will also be beneficial in other courses and will assist you in evaluating for yourself the public policies that underlie our laws and our legal system.

Frank A. Schubert

I

Introduction

REVIEW TOOLS

Chapter Overview

The first chapter provides a historical overview of the law, a description of various legal theories, and an introduction to the legal process. American law is derived from four sources: (1) the common law (decisions by judges), (2) the United States Constitution and individual state constitutions, (3) federal and state statutes, and (4) administrative regulations. You will discover that law and society are inextricably linked; laws constantly change in response to a developing society.

A description of the case study method and an explanation of basic legal terminology are included to prepare you for analyzing the cases discussed in each chapter. Through this process, you will learn to identify the critical elements of a case and develop an understanding of the relationship between real-life issues and judicial remedies.

The remainder of the chapter examines the distinctions between criminal and civil law, and tort and contract law.

Key Topics

Legal theories
Objectives of law
Historical overview
Sources of American law
    Common law

COURT CASES

E. I. Du Pont de Nemours & Company, Inc. v. Christopher

Du Pont, the plaintiff, filed suit against the Christopher brothers, the defendants, alleging that they had revealed Du Pont's trade secrets by obtaining aerial photographs of Du Pont's methanol processing plant while the plant was still under construction. Du Pont sought damages and temporary and permanent injunctive relief.

The U.S. District Court denied the defendants' motions for lack of jurisdiction and failure to state an actionable claim. The defendants took an interlocutory appeal (an appeal taken some time between the commencement and the end of a suit that decides a particular issue but is not a final decision on the entire controversy) to the Fifth Circuit Court of Appeals, which held that aerial photography of the partially exposed plant constituted an "improper means" of discovering trade secrets. By so holding, the court affirmed the lower court's decision that there was an actionable claim and remanded the case to the lower court for further proceedings on the merits.

Cruzan v. Director, Missouri Dept. of Health

Cruzan lost consciousness and fell into an irreversible vegetative state as a result of an automobile accident. After six years, her parents petitioned the Missouri trial court to order the withdrawal of her artificial nutrition and hydration tubes. The petition was granted.

The state appealed, and the Missouri Supreme Court reversed, holding that an incompetent person's desire to have medical treatment withdrawn or terminated must be proven by "clear and convincing evidence."

The U.S. Supreme Court granted *certiorari* (agreed to hear the matter) and balanced the liberty interest of an incompetent person under the due process clause of the Constitution against the interest of the state. The Court concluded that the heightened standard of "clear and convincing" evidence comports with the Constitution and that the substituted judgment of a family member or close friend would not meet the standard.

Three justices dissented, arguing that an individual has a fundamental right to be free of unwanted medical intervention that cannot be outweighed by a state's general interest in preserving life. According to the dissent, if a person is incapable of rendering a decision, the right to decide must be transferred to the family or a likely proxy of the patient.

Kolender, Chief of Police of San Diego, v. Lawson

Lawson had been detained or arrested numerous times for violating a California statute that provided that people who loiter or wander on the streets were required to show "credible and reliable" identification to police officers who had a reasonable suspicion of criminal activity. Lawson brought a civil suit seeking declaratory relief, a mandatory injunction, and compensatory and punitive damages against various officers who had detained him.

The U.S. District Court ruled that the statute was unconstitutional and enjoined its enforcement because it was overly broad. The district court held that Lawson could not recover damages, however, because the officers had acted in good faith in making the detentions and arrests.

The U.S. Court of Appeals affirmed the district court with respect to the constitutionality issue, but reversed the lower court's decision on damages. The U.S. Supreme Court affirmed the court of appeals and ruled that the statute was unconstitutional on its face. The Court concluded that the statute, as construed, failed to specify what type of identification was necessary to satisfy the "credible and reliable" requirement. This failure accorded the police too much discretion and violated the due process clause of the Fourteenth Amendment.

Goss v. Lopez

Several Ohio public school students were suspended for a maximum of ten days without a hearing. The Supreme Court affirmed the lower court's ruling that the Ohio statute empowering a public school principal to suspend students without any type of hearing deprived the students of their procedural due process rights as guaranteed by the Constitution and was, therefore, unconstitutional. The Court held that students facing suspensions must be given notice and the opportunity to be heard.

Katko v. Briney

Katko, the plaintiff, trespassed in an uninhabited house owned by the defendants, the Brineys. While doing so, Katko triggered a loaded spring gun set up by defendants in the bedroom to protect their property. The state trial court entered judgment for the plaintiff and awarded him both actual and punitive damages. The defendants appealed the actual damages portion of the verdict.

The Iowa Supreme Court held that reasonable force may be used to protect property, but not such force that inflicts great bodily injury or causes death, even where the injured or deceased party violated the law by trespassing. The court found that use of a spring gun would be justified only when a trespasser was committing a felony of violence or one punishable by death, or endangering human life.

Suggs v. Norris

Suggs sued the estate of Norris for compensation relating to her services rendered in the operation of Norris's produce business. Suggs and Norris cohabited while unmarried and were also business partners. A jury found for Suggs, and the trial judge denied the defendant's motions for directed verdict and judgment notwithstanding the verdict (j.n.o.v.). The defendant appealed, arguing on public policy grounds that because Suggs and Norris were illegally cohabiting, Suggs, was not entitled to compensation under a *quantum meruit* theory, nor was the agreement Suggs alleged existed enforceable.

The North Carolina Court of Appeals upheld the lower court's decision, holding that agreements regarding finances and property of unmarried but cohabiting couples are enforceable because sexual services or promises for sexual services do not constitute consideration for the agreements. There were sufficient facts before the jury, concluded the court, to permit it to find that Suggs and Norris had a mutual understanding regarding Suggs's compensation.

REVIEW QUESTIONS*

Key Terms

In the space provided, write the letter of each term described. Not all terms are described.

a. defendant
b. common law
c. injunction
d. consideration
e. appellant
f. substantive law

g. due process
h. plaintiff
i. tort
j. procedural law
k. contract
l. appellee

*All answers to problems are given at the end of the book.

——— 1. The type of law that mandates the methods and means of enforcing legal rights

——— 2. The party in a lawsuit against whom an appeal has been taken

——— 3. The part of a contract that is an inducement to enter into the agreement

——— 4. Rights assuring fundamental fairness and protection from arbitrary or unjust governmental action

——— 5. A person or organization against whom an action is brought

——— 6. An order by the court prohibiting the action of the defendant

——— 7. Any wrongful act, not involving a breach of an agreement, for which civil action may be maintained

——— 8. A person who initiates a lawsuit

——— 9. The type of law that creates, defines, and regulates rights

——— 10. A promissory agreement between two or more parties that creates, modifies, or destroys a legal obligation

True-False Questions

In the spaces provided, write T if the statement is true; write F if the statement is false.

——— 11. Criminal proceedings are separate and distinct from civil actions, and the rules of court procedure differ.

——— 12. The due process guarantee protects citizens from unfairness in the operation of procedural law, but does not apply to substantive law.

——— 13. Every promise is a contract, even if it cannot be enforced by law.

——— 14. An appellate court may affirm, remand, reverse, or dismiss an appeal.

——— 15. A contractual duty is imposed by law, whereas a tort duty is voluntarily assumed.

——— 16. Before a defendant in a criminal case can be found guilty, commission of the crime must be proved beyond a reasonable doubt.

_____ 17. Any state constitutional provision or federal, state, or local law that conflicts with the U.S. Constitution is invalid.

_____ 18. Only individuals, not corporations or partnerships, are entitled to the protections accorded by the due process clause of the U.S. Constitution.

_____ 19. The guarantee of due process applies to every government proceeding that may interfere with property or personal rights.

_____ 20. Crimes are classified as treason, felonies, and misdemeanors, depending not on the possible sentence or punishment but on the sentence actually given.

Multiple-Choice Questions

In the spaces provided, write the letter of the response that best completes each statement.

_____ 21. In the legal sense, the term _contract_ means
   a. the tangible document that contains evidence of an agreement.
   b. any oral, written, express, or implied agreement.
   c. any legally enforceable agreement.
   d. any promise voluntarily made.

_____ 22. Which of the following is _not_ considered a fundamental substantive due process right?
   a. Contraception
   b. Health care
   c. Child rearing
   d. Education

_____ 23. The federal Constitution guarantees due process by its
   a. Fifth Amendment.
   b. Fourteenth Amendment.
   c. Fifth and Fourteenth amendments.
   d. Article II, Section 3, clause 1.

_____ 24. When an appellate court remands a case, it
   a. affirms the lower court's decision.
   b. reverses the lower court's decision.
   c. returns the case to the lower court.
   d. submits the case to a higher court.

_____ 25. The part of the law that is developed by the courts' applications of rules to controversies is called
a. common law.
b. contract law.
c. procedural law.
d. substantive law.

_____ 26. When the same act gives rise to both a criminal proceeding and a civil suit, the legal actions are
a. independent of each other.
b. coordinated by an appellate court.
c. remanded to the lower of two courts.
d. appealed to the higher of two courts.

_____ 27. A contract consists of three parts:
a. the oral, written, and implied agreements.
b. the obligations created, modified, or destroyed.
c. the intentional, unintentional, and promissory provisions.
d. the consideration, offer, and acceptance.

_____ 28. Procedural due process rules operate more restrictively in
a. criminal cases.
b. tort cases.
c. administrative cases.
d. contract cases.

_____ 29. The enactment of substantive law is the primary responsibility of
a. the executive branch of government.
b. the administrative branch of government.
c. the judicial branch of government.
d. the legislative branch of government.

_____ 30. An intentional tort
a. occurs when a party breaches a duty imposed by contract.
b. may result in a criminal action as well as a civil action.
c. occurs when a party breaches a duty imposed by voluntary agreement.
d. always involves a promissory or consensual relationship.

Completion Questions

Summarize Chapter I by filling in the blanks to complete the following statements.

31. _____ is a dynamic process that constantly changes to fit the complex situations of a developing _____.

32. Any federal, state, or local law that conflicts with the _____ is invalid.

33. The party that brings a suit is the _____; the party against whom an action is brought is the _____.

34. The party that appeals a suit is the _____; the party against whom the appeal is taken is the _____.

35. An appellate court may _____, _____, _____, or _____ an appeal.

36. The Constitution limits the powers of federal government by the _____ guarantee in the _____ Amendment. The _____ Amendment limits the power of state government.

37. Crimes are classified as _____, _____, and _____, depending on the _____ attached to the crime.

38. A _____ is a promissory agreement between two or more parties; a _____ is any wrongful act not involving a breach of agreement for which a _____ action may be taken.

39. The three parts of a contract are the _____,
_____, and _____.

40. A contractual duty is _____, whereas a tort duty is
_____.

II

The Judicial System

REVIEW TOOLS

Chapter Overview

Chapter II describes the judicial system of the United States and explores the doctrines affecting the relationship between the state and federal courts.

The bases for jurisdiction over the subject matter of the dispute, the parties, and, at times, over the property involved, are examined, along with the propriety of venue, or the location of the court in which the complaint was filed.

A more detailed look at the federal court system and the specific functions performed by the U.S. district courts, the courts of appeal, and the Supreme Court are presented, along with doctrines concerning removal of a suit from state to federal court and application of the *Erie* principle mandating when a federal court must apply the substantive law of the state in which it sits.

Key Topics

Courts
    Trial courts
    Appellate courts
State court systems
Jurisdiction
    Subject matter
    Personal

In personam jurisdiction
Jurisdiction over property
Jurisdiction by attachment
Procedural due process
Venue
Federal court system
U.S. district courts
Jurisdiction
Criminal (original)
Civil (federal question; diversity)
Removal from state to federal courts
The Erie doctrine
U.S. courts of appeals
Scope of review
U.S. Supreme Court

COURT CASES

In the Matter of the Application of Arthur Hyde RICE to Register and Confirm Title to Land Situate in Kailua, District of Koolaupoko, Oahu, City and County of Honolulu, State of Hawaii

In land court, the Bretons brought an action to cancel a lease agreement entered into with the defendant, Central Public Supply Corporation (CPS). The plaintiffs alleged that CPS breached the agreement by defaulting on payments and by vacating the premises. CPS counterclaimed and sought to rescind the lease, claiming that the Bretons, not CPS, had committed a breach of the agreement.

The land court conducted a bench trial and entered judgment for the plaintiffs. After the land court denied CPS's motion to set aside the decision, CPS appealed to the Supreme Court of Hawaii. That court, *sua sponte* (on its own initiative), dismissed the appeal and voided the judgment of the land court on the grounds that the land court lacked subject matter jurisdiction over breach of contract actions.

Calder v. Jones

Shirley Jones, a California resident and an entertainer, brought a libel suit in California Superior Court against the editor of the *National Enquirer* and the writer of an article published therein that allegedly impugned Jones's reputation. The defendants were served a summons by registered mail in Florida, where they resided and where the *National Enquirer* is published. (Most state long-arm statutes permit service of nonresident defendants by mail). Their attorney, by a special appearance in California, moved to quash the summons for lack of personal jurisdiction. The lower court granted the defendants' motion because of First Amendment concerns. The trial court believed that freedom of speech principles mitigated against requiring reporters and editors to defend the contents of published articles in distant jurisdictions.

The California Court of Appeals reversed, stating that the defendants intended to, and did, inflict injury to Jones in California. The California Supreme Court declined to hear the case, and the plaintiffs appealed to the U.S. Supreme Court.

The U.S. Supreme Court concluded that jurisdiction was proper because the "effects" of the allegedly wrongful conduct committed in Florida were intended to cause tortious injury in California. First Amendment arguments, according to the Court, are valid only with regard to substantive issues, but cannot be raised at the jurisdictional stages of a lawsuit.

In re Union Carbide Corporation Gas Plant Disaster at Bhopal, India, in December 1984

In 1984, a gas leak from a Union Carbide India Limited plant in Bhopal, India, caused more than 2,000 deaths and over 200,000 injuries. The plaintiffs brought suit against the parent corporation, Union Carbide, in U.S. District Court in New York. The defendant, Union Carbide, filed a motion to dismiss based on the doctrine of *forum non conveniens*, seeking to have the claims heard in India.

After reviewing affidavits from experts on the Indian judiciary, the lower court concluded that India's tort law was suitable to hear technologically complex matters and that adequate remedies were available to all parties in India. The court predicated its decision on the fact that almost all the witnesses and documentary evidence were located in India, that Indian law would probably govern the matter, and that access to the plant itself demanded that the case be litigated in India.

The U.S. Court of Appeals affirmed the district court's granting of the motion for *forum non conveniens*.

Ramírez de Arellano v. Eastern Airlines, Inc.

The U.S. District Court ruled as a matter of law that the plaintiffs had not satisfied the jurisdictional amount requirement for diversity jurisdiction in a federal court. The plaintiffs were a father and daughter who had purchased first-class airline tickets for a flight from Miami, Florida, to San Juan, Puerto Rico. While on board, the father was forced to move to the coach section of the plane. He claimed that he was subjected to abuse from the captain and, as a result of the incident, suffered intense humiliation and anguish, which he valued at $60,000. He also sought $200,000 in punitive damages and $100 for the difference between a first-class and a coach ticket. The daughter, a co-plaintiff, alleged that she also suffered mental anguish and humiliation in the amount of $15,000.

Eastern Airlines filed a motion for summary judgment, claiming that the amount in controversy did not reach the jurisdictional requisite. The district court agreed and granted summary judgment, stating that there was no proof that Eastern Airlines caused anything other than "momentary embarrassment." The court concluded, therefore, that "to a legal certainty any damages plaintiffs may have suffered fall far short of the required jurisdictional amount of over $10,000. . . ."

Gatch v. Hennepin Broadcasting Associates, Inc.

A radio broadcaster brought an action against a radio station for alleged illegal and unwarranted interference with his contract to conduct a talk show when the station cut his show off the air on several occasions. Upon examination of the complaint, the federal district court concluded that it did not have removal jurisdiction. There was no diversity of citizenship between the parties, and neither the complaint nor the answer raised a federal question. Where relief was not sought under federal laws or the U.S. Constitution, removal to federal court was impermissible.

Carson v. National Bank

Johnny Carson brought an action against a travel agency for invasion of privacy. The agency had used Carson's name and picture without his approval to promote a trip to Las Vegas. The U.S. District Court found that under Nebraska law, an individual has no right to control the use of his name or image. The court of appeals affirmed the entry of judgment for defendants, noting that even though Nebraska law differed from most other states, the Nebraska Supreme Court had not indicated any move toward changing its laws.

REVIEW QUESTIONS

Key Terms

In the spaces provided, write the letter of each term described. Not all terms are described.

a. *in rem* jurisdiction
b. appellate court
c. *forum non conveniens*
d. diversity jurisdiction
e. *Erie* doctrine
f. venue

g. appellate jurisdiction
h. summary judgment
i. trial court

j. *in personam* jurisdiction
k. inferior court
l. jurisdiction

_____ 1. Requires a federal court to apply the statutes and precedents of the state in which it sits

_____ 2. A trial court that has limited jurisdiction as to subject matter and territory

_____ 3. Hears and decides controversies by determining facts and applying the appropriate laws

_____ 4. Jurisdiction over property

_____ 5. The location in which judicial authority is exercised

_____ 6. Reviews the proceedings of a lower court to ascertain whether it acted in accordance with the law

_____ 7. Jurisdiction over a person

_____ 8. Determination of issues by a judge as a matter of law where no factual disputes exist

_____ 9. The power or authority of a court to determine the merits of a dispute and to grant relief

_____ 10. An exception to the general rule that a court with jurisdiction has both the right and the duty to exercise it

True-False Questions

In the spaces provided, write T if the statement is true; write F if the statement is false.

_____ 11. The judicial branch of government has the power to establish and change courts as long as its actions are not in violation of a constitutional provision.

_____ 12. For most litigants, the U.S. courts of appeals are the ultimate appellate tribunal of the federal system.

_____ 13. Failure to object at trial usually results in a waiver of the right to raise the matter on appeal.

_____ 14. In criminal cases the defendant alone may appeal; the prosecution usually does not have that right.

_____ 15. Any civil action brought in a state court may be removed by the defendant to a federal district court if the district court has jurisdiction.

_____ 16. The United States is divided into fifty-one circuits, with one court of appeals sitting in each circuit.

_____ 17. Probate courts, small claims courts, and traffic courts are examples of state courts with limited subject matter jurisdiction.

_____ 18. The U.S. Supreme Court has appellate jurisdiction but does not have the power to function as a trial court.

_____ 19. A court does not undertake to adjudicate a dispute by itself; it can do this only when someone brings a controversy before it.

_____ 20. The doctrine of _forum non conveniens_ is applied liberally and frequently.

Multiple-Choice Questions

In the spaces provided, write the letter of the response that best completes each statement.

_____ 21. The _primary_ function of trial courts is to exercise
   a. limited jurisdiction.
   b. original jurisdiction.
   c. appellate jurisdiction.
   d. intermediate jurisdiction.

_____ 22. Either the plaintiff or the defendant may appeal a decision to an appellate court in
   a. a criminal case.
   b. a civil action.
   c. both a and b.
   d. neither a nor b.

_____ 23. There can _never_ be a waiver by the parties of
   a. subject matter jurisdiction.
   b. _in personam_ jurisdiction.
   c. venue.
   d. federal common law concerning state matters.

_____ 24. The right to a trial by jury is guaranteed by
   a. Article III, Section 1, of the federal Constitution.
   b. both federal and state constitutions.
   c. the landmark case of _Erie R. Co. v. Tompkins_.
   d. section 34 of the Judiciary Act of 1789.

_____ 25. Which of the following is *not* included within the federal court system?
   a. The U.S. Civil Court
   b. The U.S. Customs Court
   c. The U.S. Claims Court
   d. The U.S. Court of Military Appeals

_____ 26. The most common reason for a court to decline to exercise jurisdiction in a civil case is
   a. a diversity of citizenship.
   b. a writ of *certiorari*.
   c. the *Erie* doctrine.
   d. the doctrine of *forum non conveniens*.

_____ 27. The U.S. courts of appeals are divided into
   a. 51 circuits including 51 district courts.
   b. 51 circuits including 94 district courts.
   c. 10 circuits including 51 district courts.
   d. none of the above

_____ 28. In civil actions, the U.S. district courts have subject matter jurisdiction over
   a. diversity-of-citizenship cases in which the amount in controversy exceeds $50,000 and is between citizens of different states.
   b. cases that involve federal questions by arising under the Constitution, laws, or treaties of the United States.
   c. both a and b.
   d. neither a nor b.

_____ 29. The majority of cases reaching the U.S. Supreme Court come from courts of appeals
   a. as a matter of right.
   b. as set forth by section 34 of the Judiciary Act of 1789.
   c. as decided in the landmark case of *Erie R. Co. v. Tompkins*.
   d. on *certiorari*.

_____ 30. A state court has what type of jurisdiction over property located within its boundaries?
   a. *In personam*
   b. *In rem*
   c. Subject matter
   d. *Quasi in rem*

Completion Questions

Summarize Chapter II by filling in the blanks to complete the following statements.

31. The fifty-one court systems in the United States are classified by

    _____. There are _____ courts and

    _____ courts.

32. _____ is the power or authority of a court to

    determine the merits of a dispute and to grant relief, whereas

    _____ refers to the place where judicial authority

    should be exercised.

33. If a case is the sort that the court is authorized to hear, the court has

    jurisdiction over the _____. If the court has

    jurisdiction over the person of the defendant, it has

    _____ jurisdiction. If the court has jurisdiction over

    property, it has _____ jurisdiction.

34. The federal court system consists of _____ courts

    exercising original federal jurisdiction, courts

    of _____ exercising intermediate federal jurisdiction,

    and the _____ sitting as the highest court.

35. A state judicial system usually includes a _____

    court to handle deceased persons' estates,

    _____ courts limited to a specified territory, and

    _____ courts limited to relatively low maximum

    amounts.

III

Civil Procedure

REVIEW TOOLS

Chapter Overview

Chapter III describes the procedures governing civil lawsuits, from hiring an attorney through a final judgment rendered by a court. The function of a summons and complaint is discussed, along with an explanation of each of the pleadings and the different types of discovery utilized in preparation for litigation. The steps of a trial are detailed, including jury selection, the rules of evidence, and the manner in which direct and cross-examination of witnesses may be conducted. Pretrial motions, motions made during a trial, and posttrial motions are explained.

Key Topics

Proceedings prior to civil trial
    Hiring a lawyer
        Informal discovery
    Notifying the defendant
    Pleadings and pretrial motions
        Complaint
        Answer
        Reply
        Discovery
        Depositions
        Interrogatories

COURT CASES

Fracasse v. Brent

An attorney discharged shortly after being retained sought a declaratory judgment stating that he was entitled to one-third interest in any damages recovered in the personal injury action brought by his former client as set forth in their contingency fee contract.

The trial court granted the former client's motion seeking dismissal of the case. On appeal, the California Supreme Court held that an attorney discharged with or without cause is entitled to recover the reasonable value of services rendered up to the time of discharge. If a contingent fee contract is involved, the court also ruled that a cause of action does not accrue until the client receives a settlement or favorable judgment, in other words, until the stated contingency occurs.

Dorsey v. Gregg

This case involves a defendant who appealed a trial court's entry of default judgment against him. The plaintiff attempted to have the defendant served, in hand, at his fraternity house. When personal service was unsuccessful, the trial court authorized alternative service on any resident member of the fraternity house and by certified mail to the home of the defendant's father.

The Oregon Court of Appeals reversed the trial court, concluding that alternative service should not have been allowed since no attempt was made to locate the defendant at his dwelling. The trial court, therefore, lacked personal jurisdiction over the defendant.

Meyers v. Ramada Hotel and Operating Co., Inc.

The plaintiff, who was sexually assaulted in her hotel room, brought suit in U.S. District Court against the hotel for negligent security. The district court granted the hotel's motion for summary judgment, concluding that the hotel did not owe a duty to the plaintiff since the attack was unforeseeable. The plaintiff appealed to the U.S. Court of Appeals, which reversed, holding that a jury trial was required because the plaintiff had raised a genuine issue of material fact about the issue of foreseeability.

Downey v. Dixon

The plaintiff-appellant, Downey, sued Dixon and his employer, Starnes, for negligence as a result of an automobile accident. Dixon and Starnes refused to respond to the plaintiff's propounded interrogatories, and Dixon failed to attend his deposition.

The plaintiff moved the trial court for sanctions, either an order striking Dixon's answer to the complaint or, alternatively, an order denying Dixon the right to testify at the trial. The court did not impose either requested sanction but instead fined Dixon $50.

The matter went to trial, and the jury found for the defendants. The plaintiff appealed, and the South Carolina Court of Appeals reversed the judgment and remanded for a new trial. The appellate court concluded that the plaintiff was not accorded the rights of discovery as set forth by the Rules of Civil Procedure, and that a mere $50 fine did not serve as a deterrent for failing to submit to discovery.

Alexander v. Chapman

In this medical malpractice action, a widow and her son sued a doctor and the clinic with which he was associated for failing to diagnose and prevent the death of the husband/father. After a seven-day trial, the jury returned a verdict for the defendants, and a judgment was entered to that effect.

During the trial, the defendants' attorney repeatedly violated the Rules of Civil Procedure by asking leading questions on direct examination and disobeying the court's pretrial order prohibiting him from mentioning certain topics during the trial.

The plaintiffs appealed to the state supreme court, which held that the trial court had abused its discretion in failing to deal with the attorney's trial tactics. The judgment was reversed and the case remanded for a new trial.

CBS, Inc. v. Cobb

In this matter, CBS and a reporter, Victoria Corderi, sought an emergency writ of *certiorari* to quash a subpoena authorized by the lower court that ordered the release of an unpublished videotape of Corderi's interview with Bobby Joe Long, a criminal defendant then on death row. Long's murder conviction had been reversed and, during his new trial, portions of the interview, which had been broadcast, were used by the prosecution. Long subpoenaed the interview in its entirety.

Claiming a First Amendment privilege not to divulge sources, CBS and Corderi sought to quash the subpoenas. Their motion was denied, and they appealed.

The Florida appellate court held that Long met the three criteria used to determine whether disclosure of a journalist's source is necessary: relevancy, lack of alternative sources, and a compelling interest in the information. The court concluded that "Long's constitutional right to defend himself outweighs the constitutional right of CBS to withhold journalistic work product. . . ."

Cody v. Atkins

Cody brought suit for injuries allegedly sustained in an automobile collision between her car and defendant Atkins's pickup truck. The case was tried by a six-person jury. At the close of the defendant's case, the plaintiff-appellant moved for a directed verdict which was denied by the court. The jury returned a verdict in favor of Atkins, and the court entered judgment accordingly.

After trial, Cody motioned the court for a judgment notwithstanding the verdict (J.N.O.V.) and for a new trial. The trial court denied both motions, and Cody appealed to the state supreme court. That court ruled that the defendant's evidence had been sufficient to raise a jury question regarding negligence and that the trial court did not abuse its discretion in denying Cody's posttrial motions.

Newhouse v. Farmers National Bank

This action arises out of the Newhouses' purchase of real estate for $3,000 at a foreclosure sale held at the county sheriff's office. The foreclosing bank's attorney had prepared and delivered the notice announcing the sale to the local newspaper, where it was published. Approximately one-half hour after the sale was completed, the bank's attorney showed up and unsuccessfully attempted to tender a $34,200 bid for the property. As a result, the bank filed a motion to set aside the sheriff's sale, citing mistake on the attorney's part as to the time of the sale and inadequacy of the purchase price.

The bank then filed a motion for summary judgment, which was granted by the lower court. The Newhouses appealed, and the Indiana appellate court reversed, holding that a genuine issue existed about the inferences that could be drawn from the conflicting evidence. Summary judgment, therefore, was improperly granted.

REVIEW QUESTIONS

Key Terms

In the spaces provided, write the letter of each term described. Not all terms are described.

a. *subpoena duces tecum*
b. summary judgment
c. privilege
d. subpoena
e. directed verdict
f. prayer for relief

g. *voir dire*
h. interrogatories
i. hearsay rule
j. special verdict
k. execution
l. *res gestae*

_____ 1. Directs a witness to appear and testify in court

_____ 2. Directs the sheriff to seize and sell the property of a defendant who does not voluntarily pay money damages specified in a judgment

_____ 3. Prevents the compelling of testimony in a criminal trial

_____ 4. Determines each juror's qualifications for duty under the appropriate statute

_____ 5. Admissible hearsay evidence that consists of a person's spontaneous declarations uttered simultaneously with the occurrence of an act

_____ 6. Demands that the court award money damages or other remedies that the plaintiff may seek

_____ 7. Disposes of controversies prior to trial when the material facts cannot be proved

_____ 8. A judge's decision after the close of evidence that the case is so clear that reasonable people could not disagree on the result

_____ 9. Excludes evidence not proceeding from the personal knowledge of the witness

_____ 10. Questions that the parties to the case must answer in writing and under oath

True-False Questions

In the spaces provided, write T if the statement is true; write F if the statement is false.

_____ 11. The complaint is prepared by the plaintiff, and the answer and the reply are prepared by the defendant.

_____ 12. Expert witnesses are subject to the hearsay evidence rule, and they can testify only to what they personally have heard or seen.

_____ 13. Great latitude in pretrial discovery is likely to lead to a pretrial settlement.

_____ 14. If a motion for nonsuit is granted, the case is over and the defendant wins.

_____ 15. If settlement conferences prove successful, the judicial machinery is set in motion.

_____ 16. The tools of discovery include interrogations and the _voir dire_.

_____ 17. In granting a motion for judgment notwithstanding the verdict (j.n.o.v.), the judge decides that the jury is capable of reaching a reasonable conclusion.

_____ 18. A _subpoena duces tecum_ has the same general effect as a prayer for relief.

_____ 19. A standard summons warns that judgment will be rendered against the defendant unless certain action is taken within a stated time.

_____ 20. A motion for judgment on the pleadings raises only issues of law and assumes that the allegations of both parties are admitted.

Multiple-Choice Questions

In the spaces provided, write the letter of the response that best completes each statement.

_____ 21. The first requirement of admissibility is
   a. the hearsay evidence rule.
   b. materiality.
   c. relevancy.
   d. privilege.

_____ 22. The court as a passive adjudicator of controversies
   a. acts as an arena of first resort.
   b. neither initiates nor encourages litigation.
   c. uses appropriate procedural mechanisms to trigger an exploratory conversation.
   d. refrains from aiding pretrial discovery.

_____ 23. Which of the following is *not* a tool of discovery?
   a. Petitions
   b. Interrogatories
   c. Depositions
   d. Mental examinations

_____ 24. The defendant's constitutional right to be served with a summons in time to take action in defense is guaranteed by the
   a. due process clause.
   b. Second Amendment.
   c. free exercise clause.
   d. pretrial discovery clause.

_____ 25. The objective of a *voir dire* is
   a. to prove the materiality of the facts.
   b. to uphold the hearsay evidence rule.
   c. to challenge the cause as peremptory.
   d. to secure an impartial jury.

_____ 26. A defendant who can document the falsity of the material facts necessary to prove the plaintiff's case would move for a
   a. demurrer.
   b. summary judgment.
   c. judgment on the pleadings.
   d. directed verdict.

_____ 27. Which of the following is *not* a possible course for a dissatisfied party after the verdict has been rendered?
a. A motion for judgment notwithstanding the verdict
b. A new trial
c. A prayer for relief
d. Relief from judgment

_____ 28. Which of the following is an objectionable leading question?
a. "Under what circumstances did you last see this gun?"
b. "Did you visit the defendant in the hospital on March 3?"
c. "What is the basis of your expertise?"
d. "How would you characterize the ambulance driver?"

_____ 29. A default judgment may be entered against a defendant who
a. has lost the case, but fails to pay money damages awarded.
b. has been served properly with a summons, but then files a demurrer.
c. has been served properly with a summons, but fails to do anything.
d. files an immaterial counterclaim against the plaintiff.

_____ 30. Which of the following is not a basis for an attorney's fee?
a. Hourly rate
b. Retainer
c. Percentage of damages recovered
d. Lien

Completion Questions

Summarize Chapter III by filling in the blanks to complete the following statements.

31. Procedural _____ are intended to give each party to the controversy full access to as many facts as possible before the beginning of _____. As a passive adjudicator, the court neither initiates nor encourages _____.

32. A meeting between a plaintiff and an attorney before they are contractually bound to each other is known as an _____ conversation. A meeting between the plaintiff's lawyer and the defendant's lawyer to discuss a reasonable

solution to the dispute is referred to as a _____ conference.

33. The purpose of the _____ is formal notification that a lawsuit has been initiated against the defendant. The purpose of the _____ is to make the suit a matter of public record and to apprise the defendant of the nature of the claims.

34. The pleadings consist of the _____, _____, and _____.

35. The defendant's lawyer can challenge the legal sufficiency of the complaint by filing a motion to _____ or a _____. In order to weed out meritless cases before trial, either party may make a motion for a _____ judgment or a motion for a judgment on the _____.

36. The tools of _____ are depositions, interrogatories to the parties, production of documents, physical and mental examinations, and requests for admissions. A deposition may be _____ or _____. Questions that can be submitted only to the parties to the case, not to witnesses, are called _____.

37. A _____ examination is conducted to determine each juror's qualifications for duty under the appropriate statute, as well as any grounds for a challenge for _____ or information on which to base a _____ challenge.

38. A witness who does not voluntarily appear to testify may be ordered by means of a _____ to appear in court. A court may order a witness to produce a document by issuing a _____. A witness who does not obey these orders may be punished for _____ of court.

39. The rules of evidence apply to both jury and nonjury trials, although they are applied less strictly in a _____ trial. Facts that are not essential to the right of action are called _____. Evidence may also be excluded because a _____ exists—for example, the confidentiality of information exchanged between an attorney and client.

40. The _____ rule excludes evidence derived not from the personal knowledge of the witness but from the repetition of what was said or written outside court by another person. Among exceptions to this rule are _____, based on the belief that a statement made instinctively at the time of an event is likely to be truthful.

41. If the defendant's attorney believes that the plaintiff was unable to substantiate essential allegations adequately, the defendant may make a _____ for nonsuit. At the end of the presentation of evidence, but before the issues are submitted to the jury, either party may make a motion for a _____ verdict. If either motion is successful, the moving party _____ the dispute.

42. After the verdict has been rendered, a party not satisfied with it may move for a new _____, for judgment _____ the verdict, or for _____ from judgment.

43. If the defendant does not voluntarily pay money damages specified in a judgment, on application of the winning party, the court clerk issues an _____ directing the sheriff to seize and sell the defendant's property. In the alternative, the plaintiff may have a _____ placed on the defendant's property.

IV

Limitations in Seeking Relief

REVIEW TOOLS

Chapter Overview

Chapter IV identifies certain limitations in seeking judicial relief. A court is empowered to adjudicate matters that present a real and definite dispute or, in federal parlance, a "case or controversy." The parties must have "standing," or a legally sufficient personal interest in the suit. For a court to render a valid decision, it must have jurisdiction, the suit must be brought within a statutorily prescribed time period (statute of limitations), and the matter must not have been previously decided.

This chapter also explores when the law provides immunity from a legal action to the government, its officials, and other institutions and individuals.

Key Topics

Case or controversy
　　Standing
Mootness
Political questions
Act of state doctrine
Statute of limitations
Res judicata
Immunity from legal action
　　Sovereign immunity
　　Immunity of government officials

Charitable immunity
Immunity among family members
Immunity through contract

COURT CASES

Richards v. Cullen

Richards, an inmate, brought a declaratory judgment action pursuant to state statutory law and the Eighth Amendment to the U.S. Constitution to invalidate a prison rule allowing double celling of prisoners. The lower court concluded that Richards did not have standing to challenge the rule and dismissed the action.

Richards appealed. The Wisconsin Court of Appeals affirmed the lower court's ruling that Richards did not have standing under the applicable statute, which accords standing if a rule "interferes with or impairs, or threatens to interfere with or impair . . . legal rights and privileges. . . ." The court also agreed that Richards did not establish an Eighth Amendment violation.

DeFunis v. Odegaard

The plaintiff challenged the constitutionality of the admissions policy of the University of Washington Law School, claiming that he was discriminated against on the basis of race, which violated the equal protection clause of the Fourteenth Amendment.

After the trial court granted the plaintiff's requested injunction, he was admitted to the school. The state supreme court reversed. The U.S. Supreme Court granted *certiorari* and stayed the state supreme court's judgment pending final disposition of the case. DeFunis was in his last quarter of law school when the Supreme Court finally heard the matter. The Court found that regardless of any decision it rendered on the merits, the plaintiff would still graduate and, thus, the case was held to be moot.

Belk v. United States

Former Iranian hostages and two of their wives filed suit against the United States in the United States Claims Court seeking compensation because the Algiers Accord deprived them of the right to sue Iran for injuries sustained while being held hostage. The claims court granted the government's motion for summary judgment and dismissed the suit on the ground that the complaint raised a political question, which the court is not permitted to entertain, and that the government's action did not constitute a "taking," which requires just compensation.

The U.S. Court of Appeals for the Federal Circuit affirmed the lower court's decision, which stated that the case "involves a policy decision made by the President during a crisis situation" and therefore was not "susceptible to judicial review."

Marybeth Atkins v. Jiminy Peak, Inc.

This case involves a personal injury action brought by an injured skier against a ski area operator, who, plaintiff claimed rented her defective ski equipment. The complaint was filed December 5, 1984, and the accident occurred March 20, 1982.

The defendant moved for summary judgment on the ground that the action was barred by the statute of limitations. The trial court granted the motion, and the case was transferred to the Supreme Judicial Court on its own motion.

The plaintiff argued on appeal that because her suit was brought against the defendant in his capacity as the rentor of equipment, not as the operator of a ski resort, the one-year statute of limitations did not apply.

The state supreme court affirmed the lower court's ruling. It stated that the one-year statute of limitations applied to all personal injury actions brought by skiers against ski area operators arising out of ski injuries.

Caporino v. Lacasse

The plaintiff brought a small claims action against the defendant in February 1984 for failing to maintain his premises in a safe condition and won a money judgment in the amount of $163.95. Five months later, the plaintiff brought a second lawsuit in district court alleging the same set of circumstances.

The defendant made a summary judgment motion, contending that the second suit was barred by the doctrine of *res judicata*. The district court granted the motion, and the superior court affirmed. On appeal, the state supreme court affirmed and stated that the doctrine of bar and merger (a branch of *res judicata*) prohibits relitigation of the same cause of action between the same parties when a valid final judgment on the matter has previously been rendered.

Forrester v. White

The plaintiff was formerly employed by a state court judge as a probation officer. She filed a civil rights lawsuit in U.S. District Court against the judge, claiming that he had demoted and discharged her because of her sex. The U.S. District Court granted summary judgment to the judge on the ground that he was absolutely immune to such a suit. The plaintiff appealed to the U.S. Court of Appeals, which affirmed the district court. The plaintiff filed a petition for a writ of *certiorari*, which was granted by the U.S. Supreme Court. The Supreme Court reversed, ruling that while judges have traditionally enjoyed absolute immunity from civil liability for their judicial acts, they do not enjoy absolute immunity for administrative decisions.

Thompson v. Mercy Hospital

This negligence action was brought by a mentally retarded woman employed by the hospital. The plaintiff claimed that the hospital did not train her properly and that she sustained injuries as a result. The hospital filed a motion to dismiss, invoking the charitable immunity defense, which the superior court granted.

On appeal, the Supreme Judicial Court of Maine vacated the lower court's judgment and remanded for the entry of summary judgment in favor of the plaintiff. The appellate court concluded that since the hospital received less than one percent of its annual revenue from charitable sources, it could not benefit from the charitable immunity defense.

Hurst v. Capitell

A minor girl, through her grandmother, brought suit against her stepfather for sexual abuse and against her natural mother for allowing the abuse to happen. The trial court dismissed the action against the mother and granted summary judgment to the stepfather based on the parental immunity doctrine, which barred children from bringing personal injury suits against their parents.

The minor appealed. The Supreme Court of Alabama reversed the lower court's decisions for both the stepfather and mother and remanded the case for a trial. The court expressly created an exception to the parental immunity doctrine for sexual abuse cases.

Gimpel v. Host Enterprises, Inc.

The plaintiff brought suit in U.S. District Court for injuries received when he fell off a bicycle rented from the resort. The plaintiff claimed that the defendant failed to maintain and inspect the bicycle's brakes properly. The defendant moved for summary judgment based on the preprinted rental agreement, signed by the plaintiff, which released the defendant from all liability arising from the rental. The trial judge applied Pennsylvania law and held that the exculpatory clause contained within the rental agreement was valid and enforceable. Summary judgment, therefore, was granted.

REVIEW QUESTIONS

Key Terms

In the spaces provided, write the letter of each term described. Not all terms are described.

a. demurrer
b. privity
c. *res judicata*
d. statute of limitations
e. standing
f. ripeness

g. *respondeat superior*
h. proprietary function
i. sovereign immunity
j. moot case
k. political question
l. collusive case

_____ 1. Exists when the government engages in activity that is usually carried on by private individuals or that is commercial in character

_____ 2. A controversy already judicially decided

_____ 3. A case that will not be heard by the courts because the questions no longer involve the litigants before them

_____ 4. Exists when there is a relationship between two people that allows one not directly involved in the case to take the place of the one who *is* a party

_____ 5. A fundamental principle of the common law that a nation or state is exempt from being sued without its express consent

_____ 6. Establishes that a legally sufficient personal interest in a dispute exists, entitling an individual or entity to bring a lawsuit

_____ 7. Prevents a court from adjudicating a claim when resolution impinges on executive and legislative branches of government

_____ 8. A time period established by a legislature within which an action must be brought on claims or rights be enforced

_____ 9. A case that will not be heard by the courts because one party is financing and controlling both sides of the litigation .

_____ 10. Exists when the subject of a controversy or government act has a direct adverse effect on the party making the challenge

True-False Questions

In the spaces provided, write T if the statement is true; write F if the statement is false.

_____ 11. The U.S. Supreme Court has always construed the case-or-controversy requirement as precluding federal courts from being advisers to the other branches of government or to anyone else.

_____ 12. By providing immunity from tort liability in situations where it is in the best public interest, the law makes an exception to the rule that there must be a remedy for every wrong.

_____ 13. If parties create their own immunities by agreeing through contract not to sue, the courts must uphold such immunities.

_____ 14. Once an action is commenced on a claim within the statutory time period, it does not matter if judgment ultimately is rendered _after_ the period of limitations has expired.

_____ 15. The principle of _res judicata_ prevents the loser from appealing the decision of a lower court to a higher court.

_____ 16. The English common law doctrine of parental immunity has gained validity and force as interpreted by U.S. courts.

_____ 17. By the Federal Tort Claims Act of 1946, the U.S. government waived its immunity for tort liability for all acts of federal employees.

_____ 18. An exception to the mootness rule is made when the issue before the court is capable of repetition.

_____ 19. When privity exists, the executor of a person who dies after a lawsuit has concluded may bring another suit for the same cause of action.

_____ 20. The statutory period is counted from the day when a suit first could have been maintained, and it generally continues to run until the time period is exhausted.

Multiple-Choice Questions

In the spaces provided, write the letter of the response that best completes each statement.

_____ 21. In 1946 the federal government waived its immunity from tort liability by passing the
   a. Sovereign Discretionary Function Act.
   b. Sovereign Proprietary Function Act.
   c. Federal Employee Tort Act.
   d. Federal Tort Claims Act.

_____ 22. Traditionally, husbands and wives have been immune from liability for torts committed against their spouses because
   a. spouses are considered to be separate legal entities.
   b. privity does not exist between spouses.
   c. personal tort actions between spouses would disrupt the peace and harmony of the home.
   d. courts generally do not have the power to decide questions that are moot.

_____ 23. Where the parties are of one interest and seek the same relief, the case is
   a. moot
   b. collusive.
   c. collateral.
   d. proprietary.

_____ 24. A controversy is appropriate for judicial determination only when
   a. the principle of _res judicata_ applies.
   b. there is a definite and real dispute.
   c. the dispute does not arise from governmental action.
   d. an exception is made to the mootness rule.

_____ 25. Once the statute of limitations has run,
   a. the defendant may plead the statute as a defense.
   b. the defendant loses the cloak of immunity.
   c. the plaintiff must prove an identity of parties and an identity of issues.
   d. only the plaintiff may appeal.

_____ 26. For _res judicata_ to apply,
   a. the parties to a successive suit must be in privity with the parties to the original suit.
   b. the cause of action in the first case must be the same the second time litigation is attempted.
   c. either a or b.
   d. both a and b.

_____ 27. Which of the following may *not* serve to toll the running of the statute of limitations?
a. Imprisonment
b. Insanity
c. *Respondeat superior*
d. War

_____ 28. An important consideration for courts in determining whether to enforce immunity through contract is
a. the relative bargaining power of the parties.
b. the appellee's demurrer.
c. whether or not a collateral estoppel is operative.
d. suspension of the case-or-controversy requirement.

_____ 29. A final decision by a competent court on the merits concludes the litigation of the parties and
a. prevents the loser from appealing the decision to a higher court.
b. tolls the running of the statute of limitations.
c. abolishes the case-or-controversy requirement.
d. constitutes a bar to a new suit.

Completion Questions

Summarize Chapter IV by filling in the blanks to complete the following statements.

30. To be within the federal judicial power, a matter must be a

_____ or _____ as required by Article III, Section 2, of the Constitution. Many state constitutions follow the federal Constitution and do not provide for the rendering of _____ opinions.

31. _____ cases are outside the judicial power, since there is no case or controversy. Mootness is an aspect of

_____ in that there is no reason to try a case unless there has been some direct _____ effect to some party.

32. The time period within which an action must be brought is established by the _____ and is known as the _____. Occurrence of certain conditions may _____, or suspend, the running of the statutory time period.

33. The justification for the principle of _____ is that there must be an end to litigation. For this principle to apply, there must be an identity of _____ as well as an identity of _____.

34. The law provides _____ from tort liability in situations in which it is in the public interest. For example, _____ prevents one from suing the government without its express consent, and parties may agree through _____ not to sue each other.

35. Regarding sovereign immunity, courts have drawn a distinction between functions of the government that are _____ (such as military actions in time of war) and those that are _____ (such as providing services that a commercial corporation may perform). Governmental officials are immune from tort liability only in the performance of _____ duties.

36. Regarding immunity among family members, courts have been developing exceptions to the common law immunity between _____ and _____, who are now considered to be separate legal entities. In addition, _____ immunity is gradually being eroded. It is recognized that an _____ minor child can enforce a contract or property right against a parent.

V

Judicial Decision Making

REVIEW TOOLS

Chapter Overview

Judicial decisions create a body of law known as the common law. Numerous rules and doctrines govern courts in rendering decisions. This chapter explores those rules and doctrines, including *stare decisis*, the practice of adhering to precedent. Only the specific holding of a case, set forth in a reported, published decision, constitutes precedent.

The chapter also describes how courts determine which state or country's substantive laws apply in tort and contract disputes when the incident giving rise to a lawsuit implicates different states or nations.

Key Topics

Following precedent
   Stare decisis
   Rule of the case
   Requirements for a precedent
   Retroactive and prospective
      application
   Absence of precedent
Recognizing foreign law
   Conflict of laws
      Tort cases
      Contract cases

Full faith and credit
Comity

COURT CASES

State v. Butler

The defendant was convicted of aggravated assault, and he appealed, claiming that during the trial, some of his prior inconsistent statements made to the police without *Miranda* warnings were used by prosecutors. The Supreme Court of Ohio held that the Fifth Amendment protection against compulsory self-incrimination does not operate to exclude the prosecution's use of voluntary statements of an accused, made to police without *Miranda* warnings, for the sole purpose of impeaching credibility on cross-examination.

Camden I. Condominium Association, Inc. v. Dunkle

The plaintiffs brought suit in U.S. District Court to recover interest income earned prior to 1981 while the plaintiff's funds were on deposit with the Palm Beach County Clerk of Court. The plaintiffs had deposited the funds pursuant to a Florida statute that the U.S. Supreme Court in *Beckwith*, decided in 1981, found to be unconstitutional. The defendant made a motion to dismiss on the ground that the Supreme Court's decision should be applied prospectively and not retroactively. The trial court granted the defendant's motion and dismissed the complaint.

The plaintiffs appealed to the U.S. Court of Appeals for the Eleventh Circuit. The court of appeals vacated the district court dismissal order and remanded the case for a determination of whether a retroactive application of *Beckwith* would result in "substantial inequity."

Strunk v. Strunk

The mother of an incompetent 27-year-old man petitioned the court for authority to allow a kidney from her son to be transplanted into her 28-year-old son, who was suffering from a fatal kidney disease. The state circuit court adopted the findings of the county court, which held that the operation was necessary and that the incompetent's well-being would be more severely jeopardized by the death of his brother than by surgery.

On appeal, the Kentucky Court of Appeals affirmed the lower court's decision, holding that a court of equity had the power to authorize the surgery when the findings of the lower court were based on substantial evidence.

Hubbard Manufacturing Co., Inc. v. Greeson

Greeson, an Indiana resident, filed a wrongful death action, as the administrator of her husband's estate, against the defendant, an Indiana corporation, which manufactured lifts used to clean streetlights. The plaintiff's husband, who was also an Indiana resident, died while using one of the defendant's lifts in Illinois.

The defendant moved the trial court for a ruling on whether the product liability laws of Indiana or Illinois were applicable. The court determined that Indiana substantive law applied. The state court of appeals concluded otherwise and held that under Indiana conflicts of law rules, Illinois law must be used.

The plaintiff appealed to the Indiana Supreme Court. That court vacated the decision of the court of appeals and remanded the case to the trial court with instructions to apply Indiana substantive law. In so holding, the Indiana Supreme Court determined that the significant relationship approach governed, rather than the rigid *lex loci delicti commissi*, since all parties resided in Indiana and the situs of the tort bore "little connection" to the action.

Apperson v. Ampad Corporation

Apperson sued his former employer in U.S. District Court in Illinois for wrongful termination, breach of contract, fraud, and attempting to place him in involuntary servitude. Ampad moved to dismiss four of the six counts in the plaintiff's complaint on the ground that they failed to state a claim on which relief could be granted—Rule 12(b)(6) of the Federal Rules of Civil Procedure. Apperson's claim that he was entitled to expect employment with Ampad beyond a three-year period was based on language contained in an acquisition agreement executed when Ampad acquired the assets of Apperson's previous employer. The agreement contained a choice of law provision stating that Minnesota law would govern the contract.

The federal district court determined that based on Illinois conflicts of law principles, Minnesota substantive law would be used to construe the contract. Based on Minnesota law, the defendant's motion for dismissal on the four counts was granted.

GNLV Corporation v. Jackson

In a Nevada state court, GNLV obtained a money judgment against defendant Jackson, a Texas resident, for a gambling debt. GNLV then filed the judgment in a Texas court. Jackson moved to permanently enjoin enforcement of the judgment because it violated Texas public policy against enforcing gambling debts. The lower court granted the requested injunctive relief.

The Court of Appeals of Texas reversed and remanded for further proceedings, ruling that regardless of Texas's public policies, Texas does not have the right to deny full faith and credit to a Nevada judgment.

Somportex Limited v. Philadelphia Chewing Gum Corporation

The plaintiff, a British corporation, filed a diversity action in U.S. District Court to enforce a default judgment obtained in England. The court entered summary judgment for the plaintiff, and the defendant, a Pennsylvania corporation, appealed. The Third Circuit Court of Appeals held that since the defendant was given the opportunity to oppose the English court's jurisdiction and failed to do so, the defendant waived its right to present substantive arguments to that court. The English default judgment was, therefore, enforceable in a federal district court under the doctrine of comity.

REVIEW QUESTIONS

Key Terms

In the spaces provided, write the letter of each term described. Not all terms are described.

a. rule of the case
b. *lex loci delicti commissi*
c. comity
d. *stare decisis*
e. holding of the case
f. consortium

g. *amicus curiae*
h. *dictum*
i. conflict of laws
j. *lex fori delicti*
k. common law
l. full faith and credit

_____ 1. The rule of law as applied to the facts of the case

_____ 2. The law of the place where an action was instituted

_____ 3. The problem presented whenever a legal controversy arises in which there is a foreign element

_____ 4. The doctrine that a rule of law that has resulted from judicial decisions generally is binding on the courts and should be followed where applicable in later cases

_____ 5. The practice by which one court follows the decision of another court on a similar question, though not bound by the law of precedents to do so

_____ 6. Law that derives its force and authority from judicial decisions, not from any express statute

_____ 7. A judicial statement concerning a point of law that is not necessary for the decision of the case in which it is stated

_____ 8. The law of the place where the wrong was committed

_____ 9. Describes the provision in Article IV, Section 1 of the federal Constitution, whereby state laws are made effective in other states

_____ 10. Those points of law decided by a court to resolve a legal controversy

True-False Questions

In the spaces provided, write T if the statement is true; write F if the statement is false.

_____ 11. Prior decisions on a point of law are binding on a future case only if the same (or substantially the same) issue is involved.

_____ 12. No mandate in international law requires one nation to give effect to the laws of another country.

_____ 13. A dissent has precedential value if appellate court judges are equally divided and the decision affirms the decision of the next-lower court.

_____ 14. The rule of the case as expressed in a court's holding becomes a precedent that guides courts in their decisions and is generally considered to be the law.

_____ 15. Once a reported judicial precedent-setting opinion is found, its effective date is the date of the events that gave rise to the suit.

_____ 16. _Stare decisis_ is not a binding rule, and a court need not feel absolutely bound to follow previous cases.

_____ 17. When judges are confronted by a novel fact situation, they must rely on their own interpretation of law and sense of justice, to create new law.

_____ 18. In deciding tort cases, most states apply the _lex fori delicti_ rule rather than _lex loci delicti commissi_.

_____ 19. Facing a conflict-of-laws problem, a court must decide which substantive law to apply, but it always follows its own procedural law.

_____ 20. A question of fact determined by a court has binding effect on a subsequent case involving a similar question of fact.

Multiple-Choice Questions

In the spaces provided, write the letter of the response that best completes each statement.

_____ 21. When the facts of a case are substantially different from previously adjudicated cases,
   a. judges face a conflict-of-laws problem.
   b. the principle of *stare decisis* does not apply.
   c. an *amicus curiae* may intervene to influence the decision.
   d. the *dictum* may be binding under the doctrine of *stare decisis*.

_____ 22. Each jurisdiction determines for itself the extent to which
   a. comity applies.
   b. *stare decisis* is applied.
   c. both a and b.
   d. neither a nor b.

_____ 23. If the place where the contract is to be performed has more connection with the transaction than does the place where the contract was made, a court would choose to apply
   a. *lex loci contractus.*
   b. *lex loci solutionis.*
   c. *lex loci delicti commissi.*
   d. comity.

_____ 24. A conflict-of-laws problem is presented when
   a. the facts of a case have occurred in more than one state or country.
   b. an event occurred in one state and the suit is brought in another state.
   c. either a or b.
   d. neither a nor b.

_____ 25. *Dictum* has no value as precedent because
   a. it is not specifically concerned with the facts of the case.
   b. it is concerned with points of law.
   c. *stare decisis* is not an absolutely binding rule.
   d. each court follows its own substantive law.

_____ 26. Article IV, Section 1 of the federal Constitution provides for
   a. *stare decisis.*
   b. rule of the case.
   c. retroactive effect.
   d. full faith and credit.

_____ 27. All states have developed their own conflict-of-laws rules for
  a. contract disputes.
  b. moot cases.
  c. *dictum.*
  d. decisions of the U.S. Supreme Court.

_____ 28. A decision of a state court of final appeal on an issue of state law is binding on
  a. lower state courts only.
  b. lower state courts and federal district courts in that state.
  c. lower state courts and other states' trial courts.
  d. all states' trial courts and appellate courts.

_____ 29. Which of the following is *not* considered when precedent is lacking in the forum state?
  a. Public interest
  b. Business usage
  c. *Stare decisis*
  d. Moral standards

_____ 30. A decision by a court without a reported opinion
  a. does not constitute a holding.
  b. does not have *stare decisis* effect.
  c. results in a conflict-of-laws problem.
  d. undermines full faith and credit.

Completion Questions

Summarize Chapter V by filling in the blanks to complete the following statements.

31. The doctrine of _____ is the basis of common law and generally is _____ on the courts. Prior decisions on a point of law are not binding when the _____ of a case are substantially different from the facts of a previously adjudicated case.

32. Only a judicial decision of the _____ of a court on a point of law expressed in connection with a _____ opinion has *stare decisis* effect.

33. Those points of law decided by a court to resolve a legal controversy constitute the _____ of the case. Judicial expressions that are not necessary to support the decision are referred to as _____ and have no value as _____ because they do not fit the facts of the case.

34. The effective date of a precedent-setting opinion is the date of the _____, not the date of the _____ that gave rise to the suit. A court has the power to declare in its opinion whether the decision should be given _____ or _____ application.

35. Inconsistencies among the laws of the various states may result in a _____ whenever a legal controversy involves a foreign element. In this situation, the court must decide which _____ law to apply, although it always follows its own _____ law.

36. In tort cases, the traditional approach is to apply the law of the place in which the wrong is committed, which is referred to as _____. All states have developed their own conflict-of-laws rules for contract disputes. Generally, the law of the state in which the contract was made, or _____, determines the validity of a contract.

37. Since each state in the United States is a distinct _____, the laws of one state have no effect, of their own force, in any other state. Article _____, Section _____ of the federal Constitution provides that "full faith and credit shall be given in each state to the public acts,

records, and judicial proceedings of every other state," provided that the judgment is not against the _____ of the home state.

38. _____ is the recognition that one sovereignty accords to the legislative, executive, or judicial acts of another. No mandate in _____ law requires one nation to give effect to the laws of another country.

VI

Judicial Remedies

REVIEW TOOLS

Chapter Overview

Chapter VI describes the different forms of judicial remedies courts may award. Those remedies are divided into two groups: common law and equitable remedies. Common law remedies are generally limited to the awarding of monetary damages, such as compensatory and punitive. Equitable remedies, awarded only when common law remedies are inadequate, include injunctions, temporary restraining orders, reformation, rescission, and specific performance.

Restitution and declaratory judgments, two other types of judicial remedies, fall into both categories, depending on the circumstances and the particular court.

Key Topics

Common law remedies
    Compensatory damages
    Punitive damages
    Nominal damages
    Liquidated damages
Equitable remedies
    Injunctions
    Reformation and rescission
    Court of conscience

Equitable maxims
Specific performance
Restitution
Declaratory judgment
Jury trial

COURT CASES

Macomber v. Dillman

The Macombers sued their doctor and a hospital association for negligence relating to a failed tubal ligation performed on Roxanne Macomber, who gave birth to a healthy, normal child following her sterilization procedure. The plaintiffs sought damages for, among other items, the costs of raising and educating the child.

The defendants moved for summary judgment, claiming that plaintiffs' complaint did not state an actionable claim. The court denied the motion and ruled that if the plaintiffs prevailed, they could recover standard damages, including child-rearing expenses.

The case was reported to the Supreme Court of Maine on a joint motion of the parties. The court held that plaintiffs did set forth a claim for negligence, but that child-rearing costs for a healthy child were not recoverable as a matter of public policy.

Volz v. Coleman Co., Inc.

The plaintiff in this case was severely burned, at the age of five, by a stream of fuel ejected by a Coleman camp stove. The plaintiff alleged that the defendant negligently designed the fuel tank filler cap. The case was tried by a jury, and the plaintiff was awarded $6.8 million in compensatory damages and $1.06 million in punitive damages. The court of appeals affirmed the awards.

The defendant appealed to the Supreme Court of Arizona, which limited its review to the issue of punitive damages. The court reversed the $1.06 million award, holding that the plaintiff had not met the standard of proving that Coleman's actions were motivated by an "evil mind."

Lakewood Creative Costumers v. Sharp

The plaintiff rented a Halloween costume to the defendant, Sharp, for $20. The rental agreement included a liquidated damages clause stating that "an amount equal to one-half the rental fee will be charged for each day the costume is returned late." Sharp returned the costume 79 days late, and the plaintiff sued in small claims court.

At a hearing before a referee, the plaintiff testified that he had lost one rental during the 79 days. The referee awarded the plaintiff $500, noting that the plaintiff's complaint sought only that amount. Sharp filed objections to the referee's report, and the matter was brought to the trial court. It entered judgment against Sharp for $400.

The Ohio appellate court held that the liquidated damages clause was invalid because it provided for a disproportionate recovery to the plaintiff and because the actual damages incurred by the defendant's breach of contract were ascertainable. The court affirmed the trial judge's judgment against Sharp, but reduced the amount to $20 for the loss of one rental, and court costs.

Gano v. School District No. 411 of Twin Falls County, Idaho

The plaintiff, a high school student, wore a T-shirt to school that showed a caricature of three high school administrators holding alcoholic beverages and acting drunk. The school district refused to allow him to wear the shirt in school. The plaintiff sought a preliminary injunction in U.S. District Court enjoining the school district from suspending him for wearing the shirt in school. The district court followed the Ninth Circuit's test for determining whether to issue a preliminary injunction and declined to grant the motion. The court ruled that the harm to the student was minimal and that he had only a "minuscule" chance of success on the case's merits, while the administrators were exercising their statutory duty of teaching students about the effects of alcohol.

Department of Transportation v. Ronlee, Inc.

Ronlee, Inc., the plaintiff, was the successful bidder on a large construction contract with the Florida Department of Transportation. Five days after signing the contract, the plaintiff notified the defendant that the bid contained a unilateral error of $317,463, still bringing it under the next lowest bid. In response, the defendant informed Ronlee that although it was aware of the error, public policy prevented modification to the contract price.

After working on the project for twenty-one months, Ronlee brought an action seeking reformation of the contract. Both parties moved for summary judgment, and the court held in favor of Ronlee, stating that the department's failure to take action regarding the error constituted inequitable conduct.

The Florida District Court of Appeals reversed, concluding that reformation is an inappropriate remedy for unilateral mistakes in public contract bids unless inequitable conduct has occurred. The court concluded that the department's silence regarding the mistake was immaterial when Ronlee opted not to withdraw its bid after discovering the miscalculation. The trial judge's order was reversed and the case remanded with an order to enter judgment for the transportation department.

Campbell Soup Company v. Wentz

George and Harry Wentz, Pennsylvania farmers, contracted to deliver a particular type of carrot to Campbell Soup. At a later date, when the carrots had become scarce, causing the market price to skyrocket, the defendants informed Campbell Soup that they would not sell the carrots at the agreed upon contract price. Campbell Soup brought suit to enjoin the defendants from selling the carrots elsewhere and to compel specific performance of the contract.

The U.S. District Court denied the plaintiff's request for equitable relief. Campbell appealed, and the U.S. Court of Appeals for the Third Circuit held that although specific performance would ordinarily have been an appropriate remedy, in this instance, the contract contained "unconscionable bargains" that equity cannot enforce.

New York Football Giants v. Los Angeles Chargers Football Club

Flowers, a senior college football player, wanted to play in the Sugar Bowl, which required him to refrain from signing with a professional team. Nevertheless, Flowers entered into a contract with the Giants with the tacit understanding that the contract would be concealed until after the game. The Giants reneged on that understanding when Flowers discussed withdrawing from the contract. In the meantime, Flowers got a better offer from the Los Angeles Chargers and formally tried to cancel the New York agreement.

The Giants brought suit, and the trial court held for the Chargers, stating that Flowers had the right to cancel the agreement because the Giants' actions had rendered the contract binding prior to the date agreed upon.

The Fifth Circuit Court of Appeals affirmed the dismissal of the complaint, reasoning that since the Giants acted deceitfully in contravention to their agreement with Flowers, the "clean hands" doctrine prevents the court from acting on the matter. The court slightly modified the judgment by concluding that in light of the equitable principles involved, the lower court should not have considered the legal issues on the merits.

Bloch v. Hillel Torah North Suburban Day School

Bloch, an elementary school child, was expelled from the school for excessive tardiness and absences. Her parents sought to enjoin expulsion and requested specific performance to educate their daughter. The trial court denied injunctive relief and both sides filed for summary judgment. The court ruled in favor of the defendant but granted the plaintiffs leave to file an amended complaint seeking money damages.

The appellate court of Illinois affirmed the decision to deny specific performance, concluding that the remedy for breach of a personal services contract is an action for money damages. Consequently, the court remanded the matter to allow the plaintiffs to file an amended complaint.

Iacomini v. Liberty Mutual Insurance Company

Iacomini, the plaintiff, contracted with Zadlo to tow, store, and repair a Mercedes-Benz automobile. Zadlo had represented himself as the owner of the car. The car, however, had been stolen, and Liberty Mutual had obtained title to the vehicle by paying the true owner's insurance claim. Upon locating the car, Liberty Mutual sought to take possession, but Iacomini refused until his storage and repair fees were paid.

Liberty Mutual brought a replevin action against Iacomini. The court granted the motion but ordered Liberty Mutual to retain possession and ownership of the car for ninety days to allow Iacomini time to initiate an action against the company for reimbursement.

The plaintiff then filed for an *ex parte* attachment, claiming $10,000 in storage fees. Shortly thereafter, Iacomini also moved to amend his complaint to add a claim for unjust enrichment. The court found for Liberty Mutual, reasoning that the plaintiff did not have either a statutory or common law lien, for he had not contracted with the true owner's knowledge, consent, or acquiescence.

On appeal, the New Hampshire Supreme Court agreed with the lower court's decision regarding the statutory or common law lien, but held that plaintiff may be entitled to restitution under principles of equity. According to the state supreme court, an equitable lien could be imposed to prevent unjust enrichment to the extent of improvements made to the property. The lower court's denial of the plaintiff's motion to amend his complaint was reversed, and the matter remanded for a new trial.

State v. Yelsen Land Company

This case was an action by the state to settle a dispute concerning title to certain tidelands, submerged lands, and particular waters in South Carolina. The state sought to enjoin the defendants from trespassing on the property and to confirm title to the land. The defendants, by way of an answer, also claimed title and sought injunctive relief. The judge, over the state's objection and on its own motion, referred all issues for trial to a master in equity. The state appealed.

The court reversed, holding that since the complaint incorporated both equitable and legal issues, the legal issues must be tried by a jury, while the equitable issues would be determined by the judge.

REVIEW QUESTIONS

Key Terms

In the spaces provided, write the letter of each term described. Not all terms are described.

a. maxims
b. compensatory damages
c. declaratory judgment
d. ejectment
e. exemplary damages
f. restitution

g. replevin
h. injunction
i. reformation
j. liquidated damages
k. nominal damages
l. adages

_____ 1. Action used to recover possession of land as well as damages for unlawful detention or possession

_____ 2. Awarded to restore a person to a previous position to prevent unjust enrichment

_____ 3. Awarded in order to punish the defendant for conduct and to deter others from similar conduct

_____ 4. Rectifies a written instrument in order that it may express the real agreement or intention of the parties

_____ 5. An order directing the defendant to act or refrain from acting in a specified way

_____ 6. Short statements used as guides in the decision-making process in disputes in equity

_____ 7. Awarded to put the plaintiff in the same financial position as before the commission of a tort

_____ 8. Court determination of the rights of the parties to a dispute; does not order any performance relative to those rights

_____ 9. Stipulated sum contained in an agreement to be paid as compensation for loss in the event of a breach of a contract

_____ 10. Action used to recover possession of personal property wrongfully taken

True-False Questions

In the spaces provided, write T if the statement is true; write F if the statement is false.

_____ 11. Equity regards substance rather than form.

_____ 12. A permanent injunction is a final solution to a dispute and may not be dissolved through subsequent judicial action.

_____ 13. For centuries, common law and equity were administered in England by two separate sets of courts, each applying its own system of jurisprudence and following its own system of procedure.

_____ 14. Punitive damages—including attorneys' fees—can be awarded in tort actions.

_____ 15. In the U.S. legal system, equitable remedies are granted only when common law remedies are inadequate.

_____ 16. A liquidated damages clause acts as a penalty to one who breaches an agreement.

_____ 17. Nominal damages are awarded when a person suffers actual harm, but the harm is minimal.

_____ 18. If restitution involves money, the amount is determined by the plaintiff's loss, not by the defendant's gain.

_____ 19. When legal and equitable issues are joined in the same suit and are tried before a jury, the judge determines the legal issues, and the jury decides the equitable issues.

_____ 20. Most courts in the United States are empowered to grant legal relief, but equitable remedies are generally limited to appellate jurisdictions.

Multiple-Choice Questions

In the spaces provided, write the letter of the response that best completes each statement.

_____ 21. There is no constitutional right to a jury trial in
a. equity cases.
b. contract cases.
c. suits at common law.
d. suits in which legal and equitable issues are joined.

_____ 22. If a mandatory injunction is issued erroneously or if the court lacks jurisdiction, the injunction
   a. is *res judicata*.
   b. becomes a temporary restraining order (TRO).
   c. is an *ex parte* injunction.
   d. must be obeyed until it is reversed.

_____ 23. Which of the following is *not* a common law remedy?
   a. A court's awarding compensatory damages
   b. A court's awarding punitive damages
   c. A court's awarding nominal damages
   d. A court's awarding specific performance

_____ 24. When there has been a breach of an agreement or an invasion of a right, but no evidence of any particular amount of loss, the court awards
   a. compensatory damages.
   b. exemplary damages.
   c. nominal damages.
   d. liquidated damages.

_____ 25. If restitution involves money, the amount is determined by
   a. the defendant's gain.
   b. the plaintiff's loss.
   c. the defendant's gain minus attorneys' fees.
   d. the plaintiff's loss minus attorneys' fees.

_____ 26. In reaching decisions, courts of equity turn to
   a. precedent.
   b. natural justice.
   c. common law.
   d. public interest.

_____ 27. The remedy of restitution is
   a. always a common law remedy.
   b. always an equitable remedy.
   c. either a or b, depending on the situation.
   d. neither a nor b, regardless of the situation.

_____ 28. Traditionally, punitive damages have *not* been awarded in
   a. antitrust cases.
   b. contract cases.
   c. libel cases.
   d. copyright infringement cases.

_____ 29. The doctrine of avoidable harm
   a. requires the plaintiff to minimize damages by reasonable effort.
   b. prevents the plaintiff from seeking punitive damages in a tort case.
   c. requires the plaintiff to seek a temporary restraining order to protect against further loss.
   d. applies only to the defendant.

_____ 30. Two common law remedies that seek restitution are
   a. reformation and ejectment.
   b. ejectment and replevin.
   c. replevin and the benefit rule.
   d. the benefit rule and reformation.

Completion Questions

Summarize Chapter VI by filling in the blanks to complete the following statements.

31. In U.S. jurisprudence, the judicial remedies that courts award in civil cases are classified either as _____ remedies or as _____ remedies.

32. Common law remedies are generally limited to the court's determination of some _____ right and the awarding of _____. Equitable remedies generally consist of the court's issuing an _____, an order directing the defendant to act or refrain from acting in a specified way.

33. A court order compelling one to do an act is called a _____ injunction, whereas one that forbids an act is a _____ injunction. An injunction may be enforced by the _____ power of the court. It must be obeyed until it is _____.

34. A _____ injunction is supposed to be a final solution to a dispute and is issued after a full opportunity to present

evidence. A _____ or _____ injunction is granted as an emergency measure before a full hearing is held. And a _____ is an *ex parte* injunction that is granted without notice to the defendant.

35. The purpose of _____ is to restore a person to a previous position to prevent unjust enrichment. If money is involved, the amount is determined by the _____ gain, not by the _____ loss.

36. Equity in the United States is that portion of remedial justice that was formerly administered in England by the court of _____. A principal deficiency of the _____ system was that it generally awarded only money damages as relief. Even today, _____ remedies are granted only when the common law remedies are inadequate.

37. A court of equity is considered to be a court of _____ in which natural justice takes priority over _____. Instead of using rules of law in reaching decisions, courts of equity use _____.

38. For the most part, trial by jury is a _____ right in suits at _____, but there is no such provision regarding _____ cases. When legal and equitable issues are joined in the same suit, the factual issues going toward the common law relief are determined by the _____, and the factual issues going toward the equitable relief are decided by the _____.

39. Usually, a common law court grants relief in the form of damages, which are classified into _____ damages, _____ damages, _____ damages, and _____ damages.

VII

Criminal Law and Procedure

REVIEW TOOLS

Chapter Overview

Chapter VII outlines the fundamental principles of criminal law and criminal procedure in the United States. The elements necessary to constitute a crime, as well as the classification of crimes, defenses, and current approaches to criminal law are explored. The criminal procedure section focuses on the constitutional guarantees that apply before trial, during trial, and at sentencing. Besides protecting an individual's rights throughout the criminal process, our legal system aims to preserve the integrity of the community.

Key Topics

Criminal law
    Historical view
    Classification of crimes
    Constitutional limitations
    Imposition of punishment
Components of a criminal offense
    Wrongful act
    Special rules
    Status crimes
    Criminal state of mind
    Strict liability

Vicarious liability
Causation
Inchoate crime
RICO
Defenses
Criminal procedure
Proceedings prior to trial
Arrest
Investigatory detentions
Custodial interrogation
Searches and seizures
Bail
The right to an attorney
Lineups
Preliminary hearing and grand jury
Arraignment
Criminal trial
Trial by jury
Fair and public trial
Right to a speedy trial
Prosecution
Sentencing
Appeal and *habeas corpus*

COURT CASES

Loving v. Commonwealth of Virginia

In 1958, the Lovings, an interracial couple, were married in the District of Columbia, although they were both residents of Virginia. Shortly after returning to Virginia, they were indicted and convicted of violating the state's miscegenation statutes. The Lovings filed a motion in the state court to vacate the judgment and set aside their sentences on the ground that the statutes were unconstitutional. The judge denied the motion, and the plaintiffs appealed to the Supreme Court of Appeals of Virginia.

In the meantime, prior to the state judge rendering a decision, the plaintiffs filed a class action suit in the U.S. District Court. The federal court continued the case so that the Lovings could present their claims to the highest state court. That court upheld the miscegenation statutes.

The U.S. Supreme Court reversed the convictions and expressly ruled that the Virginia statutes were predicated upon "invidious racial discriminations" and thus violated the equal protection clause and the due process clause of the Constitution.

People v. Shaughnessy

The defendant, while a passenger in an automobile, was driven onto private property, where she was stopped and charged with violating an ordinance prohibiting entry onto private property without the owner's permission. At the close of her trial, the defendant moved to dismiss on the grounds that the applicable ordinance was unconstitutional.

The court dismissed the case, but not on constitutional grounds. Instead, the court held that since the defendant was merely a passenger in the automobile, her presence on the private property was not voluntary and, therefore, she could not be held criminally responsible.

State v. Gordon

The defendant, Gordon, escaped from authorities in Vermont. While in Maine, he and a friend experienced engine trouble and began to look for another vehicle. They spotted a Chevelle with keys in it. The friend got into the car, pointed a gun at the car's owner, and he and Gordon told the owner that they would "take care of [the car] and get it back as soon as possible." The defendant was charged with armed robbery and, in a separate indictment, with assaulting a police officer (based on a later incident).

A jury found the defendant guilty of armed robbery. He appealed, contending that since he intended to return the Chevelle, he did not have the specific intent necessary to constitute the crime. The Supreme Judicial Court of Maine denied Gordon's appeal. It ruled that the jury could have found that the defendant's indifference regarding the return of the automobile indicated the specific intent to deprive the owner of his property permanently.

Commonwealth v. Berggren

The defendant, while operating a motorcycle, failed to stop when pursued by a marked police cruiser for speeding. While entering an intersection, the cruiser's wheels locked and it hit a tree, resulting in the police officer's death. The defendant was charged with negligent vehicular homicide.

Prior to trial, the district court granted the parties' joint motion to report the question of whether the facts would support a conviction pursuant to the applicable statute. The report was transferred to the supreme judicial court on its own motion. It held that the standard of proximate causation in tort law is the standard to be applied to the criminal statute at issue. Therefore, since the officer's death was a foreseeable consequence of the defendant's actions, the court concluded that a conviction for negligent vehicular homicide could be supported.

United States v. Scott

Scott was convicted in U.S. District Court of one count of conspiracy to manufacture methamphetamine and one count of manufacturing the unlawful drug. He appealed his conviction on the ground that the district court refused to instruct the jury on the defense of coercion. Scott asserted that a co-defendant forced him to commit the crimes under fear of his own death or the death of a family member.

The U.S. Court of Appeals for the Tenth Circuit determined that Scott had a reasonable opportunity to escape the threatened harm and, therefore, he failed to satisfy one of the three criteria necessary for proffering a coercion defense. As a result, the appeals court affirmed the lower court's denial of the defendant's request for an instruction on the coercion defense.

Draper v. United States

A reliable informant provided a federal narcotics agent with detailed information that petitioner Draper would be arriving in Denver by train from Chicago, on one of two mornings, wearing specified clothing, and carrying three ounces of heroin. Relying on that information, the federal agent watched the train station and witnessed an individual fitting the precise description alighting from the specified train on the identified date, wearing the exact clothing described by the informant. The agent executed a warrantless arrest and, upon searching Draper, found heroin and a syringe. At trial, Draper moved to suppress the evidence, claiming that the agent's information was hearsay, which could not be used as grounds for conducting a warrantless arrest, and even if hearsay had been lawfully considered, the agent did not have probable cause or reasonable grounds to believe that Draper had committed or was committing a narcotics violation.

The U.S. Supreme Court held that the denial of the motion to suppress was proper. Since the agent personally verified all the informant's information except for whether Draper was carrying contraband, the Court concluded that probable cause and reasonable grounds to believe Draper was committing a crime existed sufficient to render Draper's arrest, and the subsequent search and seizure of the heroin, lawful.

Adams v. Williams

While alone in a high-crime area in Bridgeport, Connecticut, a police officer was approached by a known informant who relayed that an individual seated in a nearby automobile possessed narcotics and had a gun at his waist. Based on the information, the officer conducted a *Terry* stop and frisk on the individual, the respondent Williams. Specifically, the officer asked Williams to get out of his car, but instead, Williams rolled down the car window, and the officer reached inside and removed a fully loaded gun from Williams's waistband. The search incident to the arrest revealed heroin, a machete, and a second gun.

At trial, Williams contended that the stop was not justified and thus, the fruits of the search should not have been admissible. His conviction was affirmed by the Supreme Court of Connecticut, and his federal *habeas corpus* petition was denied by the U.S. District Court and by a divided panel of the Second Circuit Court of Appeals. On rehearing of the full panel (*en banc*), the circuit court reversed the conviction.

The U.S. Supreme Court, in turn, reversed the Second Circuit's decision and upheld the conviction. The Supreme Court held that the informant's tip had a sufficient "indicia of reliability" to allow the officer to investigate the situation. When Williams rolled down his window instead of getting out of the car, the officer was permitted to ensure his safety by taking the concealed weapon. Probable cause, therefore, existed to arrest Williams for unlawful possession of a weapon, and the search conducted incident to that arrest was lawful.

New Jersey v. T. L. O.

T. L. O., while a 14-year-old public high school freshman, was caught smoking in the lavatory. When questioned by the assistant vice principal, T. L. O. claimed that she did not smoke. A cursory search of her purse revealed a package of cigarettes and rolling papers. Upon seeing the rolling papers, the assistant vice principal conducted a thorough search of the purse and found a small quantity of marijuana, a pipe, empty plastic bags, and other items implicating T. L. O. in drug dealing. As a result, T. L. O. was charged with delinquency in juvenile court. Her motion to suppress the evidence was denied, and she was adjudged a delinquent. The appellate division affirmed the trial court's decision but the New Jersey Supreme Court reversed and ordered the evidence found in the purse suppressed based on Fourth Amendment grounds.

The U.S. Supreme Court granted the state of New Jersey's petition for *certiorari* and held that Fourth Amendment principles do apply to searches and seizures conducted by public school officials. School officials are state actors and are not entitled to immunity based on a *parens patriae* theory.

The Court balanced the school's need to maintain order against the student's expectations of privacy in determining whether the search was reasonable under the Fourth Amendment. The Court concluded that a school official need not obtain a warrant before searching a student suspected of violating a school rule or committing a crime. Based on a twofold inquiry about whether the search was "justified at its inception" and then "reasonably related in scope to the circumstances," the Court held that the initial search conducted on T. L. O.'s purse for cigarettes was not unreasonable, and that once the rolling papers were discovered, the search for marijuana was also legitimate. The Court reversed the state supreme court's decision to exclude the evidence from T. L. O.'s delinquency proceedings.

United States v. Salerno

Two alleged members of the Genovese family of La Cosa Nostra were arrested on multiple racketeering charges under the Racketeer Influenced and Corrupt Organizations Act (RICO). At their arraignment, the government moved to have them detained without bail pursuant to the Bail Reform Act on the ground that the safety of the community or any person would be endangered by their release. The district court granted the detention motion, but on appeal, the Second Circuit reversed, ruling that the statute was facially unconstitutional since it permitted pretrial detention on the speculation that an arrestee was likely to commit a future crime.

The U.S. Supreme Court granted *certiorari* and reversed, holding that the act did not violate either the due process clause or the Eighth Amendment. As to due process, the Court stated that pretrial detention is regulatory, not punitive, and served compelling governmental interests. The Court also rejected the argument that the Eighth Amendment's proscription against excessive bail requires only consideration of flight, not danger, in deciding whether bail should be granted.

Justices Marshall and Brennan dissented, arguing that allowing innocent people to be jailed indefinitely pending trial is tantamount to creating a police state.

REVIEW QUESTIONS

Key Terms

In the spaces provided, write the letter of each term described. Not all terms are described.

a. recognizance
b. *nolo contendere*
c. probable cause
d. plea bargaining
e. indictment
f. rehabilitation
g. incapacitation
h. right of confrontation

i. arraignment
j. retribution
k. *habeas corpus*
l. exclusionary rule
m. *actus reus*
n. *ex post facto*
o. battery
p. bill of attainder

_____ 1. A guilty plea that cannot be used later against the accused as an admission

_____ 2. Provides that evidence obtained in violation of the Constitution is inadmissible in a criminal trial

_____ 3. A theory of punishment aimed at "getting even" with offenders

_____ 4. The singling out or targeting of a particular group so as to impose punishment without a trial

_____ 5. A grand jury's written accusation against one who is believed to have committed a crime

_____ 6. Acknowledgement, in a court of law, of one's obligation to appear for trial

_____ 7. The element of a criminal offense that constitutes the wrongful act

_____ 8. Questions the legality of the incarceration of a prisoner

_____ 9. Reasonable grounds to believe that the arrestee has committed or is committing a crime

_____ 10. Offensively touching another person without his or her consent

_____ 11. A law that makes acts criminal that were not criminal at the time they were committed

_____ 12. A theory of punishment aimed at correcting offenders so that they can live according to the existing social order

_____ 13. Affords the accused and counsel an opportunity to attack the identifying witnesses' credibility

_____ 14. Satisfies the Sixth Amendment requirement that the accused "be informed of the nature and cause of the accusation"

True-False Questions

In the spaces provided, write T if the statement is true; write F if the statement is false.

_____ 15. Imprisonment represents the rehabilitation theory of punishment.

_____ 16. Statutory offenses that are *not* punishable by death or by imprisonment in a state penitentiary are usually classified as misdemeanors.

_____ 17. If you exceed the speed limit while driving a car, the government must prove both *actus reus* and *mens rea* in order to procure a conviction.

_____ 18. Federal criminal law is derived from common law and statutory law.

_____ 19. When the complaining party does not have firsthand information and relies on hearsay, the court does not issue an arrest warrant.

_____ 20. The exclusionary rule makes many of the pretrial proceedings in a criminal case insignificant.

_____ 21. Very few *habeas corpus* proceedings are successful.

_____ 22. Any treatment by a law enforcement officer that shocks the conscience of the court violates an accused's right of due process, regardless of whether the party is considered to be in custody.

_____ 23. Proximate cause is an element necessary to succeed in tort law but is not required to prove criminal liability.

_____ 24. Article I, Sections 9 and 10, of the U.S. Constitution prohibit the federal and state legislative bodies from enacting laws that impose greater punishment for a crime than when the crime was committed.

_____ 25. In sentencing a convicted felon, the judge cannot consider unsworn or out-of-court information and must reach a decision within the guidelines specified in the indictment.

_____ 26. The presumption of innocence is among the guarantees specifically mentioned in the U.S. Constitution.

_____ 27. A prosecutor who loses a case is automatically permitted to appeal on the basis of due process.

_____ 28. When formal charges are pending, an accused may not be put in a lineup before witnesses for identification unless counsel is present.

_____ 29. Being a narcotics addict is a crime.

Multiple-Choice Questions

In the spaces provided, write the letter of the response that best completes each statement.

_____ 30. A person who consents to allow a law enforcement officer to perform a search without a warrant waives the rights granted under the
a. Fourth Amendment.
b. Fifth Amendment.
c. Eighth Amendment.
d. Fourteenth Amendment.

_____ 31. Which of the following is *not* among the purposes of the right to have a speedy trial?
a. To prevent long delay that could impair the ability to defend oneself through the loss of evidence
b. To incapacitate the accused by quick imprisonment and thus protect society
c. To prevent or minimize public suspicion and anxiety connected with an accused who is yet untried
d. To protect an accused from prolonged imprisonment prior to trial

_____ 32. A writ of *habeas corpus* will be granted if the accused
a. pleads guilty or *nolo contendere* to the existing charge.
b. pleads guilty or *nolo contendere* to a reduced charge.
c. successfully shows in a full hearing that there is no legal authority for the custody.
d. successfully argues the exclusionary rule in a full hearing.

_____ 33. The gradual demise of the hands-off doctrine has resulted in
a. rapid expansion of correctional case law.
b. increased application of the exclusionary rule.
c. reduced chances for parole or pardon.
d. widespread abuse of incarcerated offenders.

_____ 34. Which of the following is *not* an inchoate crime?
a. Solicitation
b. Attempt to commit rape
c. Burglary
d. Conspiracy

_____ 35. Through plea bargaining an accused
   a. may change a plea of guilty to *nolo contendere*.
   b. may change a plea of not guilty to *res gestae*.
   c. agrees to enter a plea of guilty in exchange for concessions by the prosecutor.
   d. agrees to enter a plea of *nolo contendere* in exchange for a writ of *habeas corpus*.

_____ 36. Which theoretical justification for punishment supports strict law enforcement and assumes that crime is reduced by the fear of punishment?
   a. Retribution
   b. Incapacitation
   c. Deterrence
   d. Rehabilitation

_____ 37. Which of the following is *not* specifically guaranteed by the Constitution?
   a. "No warrants shall issue, but upon probable cause . . ."
   b. The accused shall "be informed of the nature and cause of the accusation."
   c. "The accused shall enjoy the right to a speedy . . . trial."
   d. The accused shall "be presumed innocent until . . . proven guilty."

_____ 38. The exclusionary rule relates to
   a. *habeas corpus*.
   b. the distinction between felonies and misdemeanors.
   c. recognizance.
   d. admissibility of evidence.

_____ 39. A pretrial confession is never admissible during the trial if the accused
   a. did not confess voluntarily.
   b. waived the right to the assistance of counsel.
   c. incriminated himself.
   d. was not in custody at the time.

_____ 40. Lawful arrests must be made on the basis of
   a. an arrest warrant.
   b. probable cause.
   c. incidental searches.
   d. an indictment.

Completion Questions

Summarize Chapter VII by filling in the blanks to complete the following statements.

41. The objective of _____ law is to regulate the conduct of _____ in order to maintain public order. The preservation of the integrity of the _____ is of paramount importance in determining what conduct is antisocial.

42. Crimes traditionally have been classified as _____, _____, and _____. Offenses punishable by death or by imprisonment in a state penitentiary are _____.

43. The presumption of _____ is not specifically mentioned in the Constitution, and yet it has remained unchallenged by the courts of the United States. The guarantees that deal with criminal procedure are defined primarily in the _____, _____, _____, _____, and _____ amendments.

44. The privilege against self-_____ applies to questioning outside the courtroom as well as at the trial. Any statement made by the accused during police investigation must be made _____. In addition, the Supreme Court in the case of *Miranda v. Arizona* required that certain _____ be given by the police in a custodial interrogation.

45. The police conduct _____ before witnesses for the purpose of identifying the suspect. This procedure must occur in the presence of _____ unless the suspect waives that right, once formal charges are filed.

46. The four components of a criminal offense are

    _____, _____,

    _____, and _____.

47. The common law approach to criminal law recognizes three categories of intent: _____, _____, and _____. Negligence results from unconscious

    _____.

48. An arrest for the commission of a crime may be made with or without a _____, but the officer of the law must have _____ to believe that the arrestee has committed or is committing a crime.

49. An officer conducting a _____ cannot go outside the limits set by the warrant. With the exception of some jurisdictions that allow _____ warrants, the officer must give notice of the search before _____. To secure the safety of the police officer and the custody of the suspect, an officer may conduct a limited search _____ to an arrest.

50. Employers may be held to be _____ when an employee commits an offense within the scope of his or her employment.

51. To weed out groundless or unsupported criminal charges before trial, a _____ hearing is conducted or a _____ is convened. If a grand jury believes that the evidence warrants a conviction, it will return an _____.

52. At the _____, the accused is advised of formal charges and is called on to enter a _____, which may be _____, _____, or _____.

53. To ensure the defendant's attendance in court and obedience to the court's orders and judgment, the judge sets _____ . If there is good reason to believe that the defendant will show up even in lieu of this requirement, the judge may release the accused on his or her own _____.

VIII

Contracts

REVIEW TOOLS

Chapter Overview

This chapter examines contract law. For a contract to be enforceable, (1) an offer must be made, (2) it must be accepted, (3) the agreement must be knowingly and freely consented to by competent parties, and (4) it must be supported by consideration. Chapter VIII also discusses the capacity of parties to contract, the requirement that certain types of contracts be in writing, and the available remedies for breaches of contract.

Key Topics

Nature and classification of contracts
    Valid, void, voidable, and unenforceable contracts
    Bilateral and unilateral contracts
Agreement
    Offer
        Requirements of an offer
    Termination of an offer
    Acceptance
Reality of consent
    Duress
    Undue influence
    Fraud

COURT CASES

Pluhacek v. Nebraska Lutheran Outdoor Ministries, Inc.

The plaintiffs submitted a written offer for the sale of land. The defendants counteroffered, including as a condition the approval of the full board of directors. Both parties signed the agreement. Shortly thereafter, two other parties submitted higher offers on the property. The board of directors voted to accept one of the later offers. The plaintiffs sued to compel specific performance based on the alleged contract.

The trial court dismissed the action. It found that approval by the full board of directors was a condition precedent to the formation of a contract. On appeal, the Supreme Court of Nebraska affirmed, concluding that no contract existed because the board of directors had not approved the sale to the plaintiffs. The plaintiffs, therefore, were not entitled to specific performance.

Carter v. Matthews

The appellant was awarded the equitable remedy of rescission of a contract for the sale of property on the ground of mutual mistake. She had also sought money damages for fraud, but the chancellor refused the request. Based on the refusal, she appealed to the state supreme court. The appellee cross-appealed, contending that the only basis for rescission is fraud, not mistake and, thus, the appellee argued that the chancellor had erred in granting rescission.

The state supreme court affirmed the decision of the chancellor on all grounds. The court ruled that a mutual mistake of fact is a legal basis for rescission and because the appellant could not prove reliance on the appellee's misrepresentations, the denial of money damages was not clearly erroneous.

Modern Laundry and Dry Cleaning v. Farrer

Farrer signed an employment contract with Modern Laundry that contained a restrictive covenant in the event of Farrer's termination from the company prohibiting him from working in the laundry business for a period of one year within a designated territory. After approximately fifteen years of service, Farrer left the company and opened his own laundry business. On the basis of the restrictive covenant, Modern Laundry brought suit to enjoin Farrer from operating his business. A temporary restraining order was originally issued and then dissolved following a hearing on the matter. The motion for a preliminary injunction was denied on the ground that the contract was not ancillary to Farrer's acceptance of employment.

The appellate court of Pennsylvania reversed and remanded the case to the lower court, holding that the restrictive covenant was ancillary to Farrer's taking of employment, was supported by adequate consideration, and was, therefore, enforceable.

Walker v. American Family Mutual Insurance Co.

Walker was the driver of an automobile owned by Moorman, which was involved in an automobile accident. Moorman was fatally injured in the accident. The vehicle in which they were riding was insured by the defendant insurance company. Moorman's personal representative brought suit against Walker for wrongful death. Walker was defended by American Family Mutual Insurance Company (the insurer of Moorman's vehicle), and his own insurance company, Farm and City Insurance Company.

Farm and City negotiated a settlement of the lawsuit; however, American Family Mutual refused to pay any portion of the settlement, relying on a provision in Moorman's insurance policy that excluded an insured owner from recovering for bodily injury. Farm and City then brought suit against American Family Mutual to obtain a declaratory judgment. The plaintiff wanted the trial court to declare (1) that the exclusionary clause was invalid under Iowa law, and (2) that the plaintiff was entitled to recover the settlement proceeds paid to the Moorman estate from American Family Mutual.

The trial court ruled in favor of the defendant, finding that the exclusionary clause in Moorman's insurance policy did not violate public policy. The plaintiff appealed to the state supreme court, which affirmed the trial court. It examined state legislation and case law and determined that public policy was not violated by the enforcement of the exclusionary provision of the insurance contract since the insured opted to purchase such a limited policy.

Diaz v. Indian Head, Inc.

In this action, the plaintiff sought to have declared unenforceable a provision in his employment contract that precluded competition with his former employer for eighteen months after termination. The contract expressly provided that New York law would govern. The U.S. District Court stated that New York law looked with disfavor on agreements that would prevent a talented person from engaging in his or her chosen profession.

In New York, noncompetition agreements have been held void unless the employer can demonstrate that irreparable harm would ensue by the divulging of trade secrets, or the loss of "goodwill" or important customers, or because the employee may have been "special, unique, or extraordinary." No trade secrets were involved, and the court concluded that the names of customers were known or available to all competitors. As to the third element, the court concluded that even though the plaintiff excelled, his services were not "unique." As a result, the court ruled that the plaintiff was entitled to a declaratory judgment that the noncompetition agreement was void and unenforceable.

Mulford v. Borg-Warner Acceptance Corp.

The plaintiff and the defendant had executed three written leases for office space in a single property. Prior to the expiration date, the plaintiff proposed a new three-year lease. The defendant wanted only a two-year lease on its one remaining space. The plaintiff prepared and signed the new lease. The defendant never signed the new agreement, but paid rent according to its terms. Prior to the expiration of the two years, the defendant notified the plaintiff that it was leaving the property. The plaintiff commenced suit, alleging that the unexecuted lease was a valid contract because the signed monthly checks constituted sufficient memoranda to satisfy the statute of frauds.

Borg-Warner filed for summary judgment, and the court granted its motion. On appeal, the Supreme Court of New York, Appellate Division (not the highest court) held that the rent checks did not embody the material terms of the contract and, therefore, did not satisfy the statute of frauds. The court did order the defendant to pay one additional month's rent, however, since it had stipulated that it would do so as a result of giving its termination notice one day late.

Jinright v. Russell

By oral agreement, the defendants agreed to purchase all assets and interests in the plaintiff's liquor store for $6,500. As partial payment, the defendants gave the plaintiff a check for $1,500 but then stopped payment on same. The check was signed, and on its face were written the words "For Binder on Store." Since the contract was for a sale of goods in excess of $500, and there was no actual memorandum in writing to satisfy the statute of frauds, the defendants claimed that the contract was unenforceable.

The court denied the defendants' motion for summary judgment. The appellate court in Georgia affirmed the judgment and held that under the Uniform Commercial Code, the check met the requirements of a writing because it indicated that a contract for sale was made between the parties.

Macke Company v. Pizza of Gaithersburg, Inc.

The defendants-appellees had contracted with the plaintiff's predecessor, Virginia Coffee Service, to install cold drink vending machines in six locations. Macke bought Virginia's assets, and the six contracts were accordingly assigned to Macke. When the defendants tried to terminate the contracts, Macke filed suit. The lower court held for the defendants, and Macke appealed.

The Court of Appeals of Maryland reversed the judgment as to liability. It held that absent a contractual provision, the contracts could be assigned since they were not for personal services, nor did they required particular or unique skill on Virginia's part. The case was remanded for a new trial on damages.

Castorino v. Unifast Building Products

The plaintiff's decedent was murdered by an assailant who entered her apartment through a window that either did not have a lock or that had a defective lock. The defendant, Unifast, had contracted with DCI Contracting Corporation to install windows in the decedent's apartment building.

Unifast moved for summary judgment, contending that the plaintiff could not recover on a theory of either contractual or tort liability. The trial court denied the motion without prejudice to Unifast resubmitting it after discovery determined whether the windows were manufactured and delivered in a defective condition.

Unifast appealed, and the appellate court in New York reversed and granted Unifast's motion. The court held that an intended third-party beneficiary cannot maintain a breach of contract action since the contract does not indicate an intent to allow recovery to that party for a breach. As for tort liability, the court ruled that it would be beyond "sound public policy" to hold a window supplier responsible for the "alleged consequences of an allegedly defective window locking mechanism."

Clarkson v. Orkin Exterminating Co., Inc.

Upon purchasing a house, the plaintiff continued her predecessor's contract with defendant Orkin for termite inspections and treatment. When Clarkson went to sell her house, Orkin inspected the property and issued a report that it was free of termites.

One day after Orkin's inspection, another exterminator inspected the house and found termite tunnels and water damage caused by the termites. After the repairs were made, Clarkson sued to have Orkin reimburse her for the repairs. She also asked Orkin to reinspect the house and certify that it was free of termites. Orkin refused.

A jury awarded the plaintiff money damages for breach of contract and violations of the state's Unfair Trade Practices Act, actual damages, and punitive damages for fraud. Orkin appealed, and the U.S. Court of Appeals for the Fourth Circuit reversed on the fraud and Unfair Trade Practices Act claims, but affirmed on the breach of contract claim. The court held that the failure to discover termites demonstrates a breach of contract but does not establish fraud or unfair trade practices. Since the plaintiff had not chosen to purchase Orkin's guarantee to repair property damage caused by termite infestation, she was not entitled to the cost of such repairs. The matter was remanded solely for a new determination of damages.

Anuszewski v. Jurevic

The Jurevics contracted with the plaintiff to build a home in Kennebunkport, Maine. On the date the house was to be completed, it was only half done.

After the Jurevics discharged the plaintiff, he brought an action to recover damages for the unpaid part of the contract price, or alternatively, the value of labor and materials for which he had not been paid. The Jurevics counterclaimed, claiming that Anuszewksi's work was defective and that the cost to correct the defects and finish the house included a general contractor's markup. The court refused to allow the jury to consider the markup in assessing damages on the counterclaim. After the jury awarded damages to both parties, the Jurevics appealed the denial of their motion for a mistrial, a new trial, or an additur.

The Supreme Judicial Court of Maine affirmed the judgment on the complaint but vacated the judgment on the counterclaim, reasoning that contract damages are intended to place the injured party in the same position he or she would have been in but for the breach. Therefore, the court concluded that a general contractor's markup must be considered by a jury in determining contract damages.

Hibschman Pontiac, Inc. v. Batchelor

Batchelor purchased an automobile from Hibschman Pontiac upon personal representations from the salesman, the service manager, and the vice president that the service department was "above average." Batchelor experienced numerous problems with the car, and each time he brought it to Hibschman Pontiac for repairs, the work was either done poorly or not done at all, despite assurances to the contrary. A jury trial resulted in a verdict for Batchelor. He was awarded $1,500 in damages and $15,000 in punitive damages. The state appellate court reversed the granting of punitive damages.

On appeal, the Supreme Court of Indiana held that there was sufficient evidence to warrant the jury awarding punitive damages since it could have found that elements of a common law tort, including fraud, malice, gross negligence or oppression, were "mingled" into the breach of warranty claim. The court rejected Hibschman's contention that the trial court should have directed a verdict in its favor on the issue of punitive damages.

REVIEW QUESTIONS

Key Terms

In the spaces provided, write the letter of each term described. Not all terms are described.

a. parol evidence rule
b. offer

c. bilateral contract
d. fraud

e. accord
f. consideration
g. innocent misrepresentation
h. duress

i. option contract
j. statute of frauds
k. acceptance
l. satisfaction

_____ 1. A promise that is conditioned upon a return promise, act, or forbearance being given in exchange

_____ 2. The agreement to accept something different from what was due under an original contract

_____ 3. Any unlawful constraint that forces a person's consent to an agreement that otherwise would not be made

_____ 4. Holds that prior agreements or terms not contained in the writing of a written contract are not admissible in court to prove any matter within the contract

_____ 5. An intentional act of deception used by one individual to gain an advantage over another

_____ 6. That which is bargained for and given in exchange for another's promise

_____ 7. Binds the offeror to hold an offer open, usually for a stipulated time

_____ 8. An expression of agreement by the offeree to be bound by the terms of the offer

_____ 9. Require that certain contracts be in writing to be enforceable

_____ 10. The offer of something different from what was due under an original contract

True-False Questions

In the spaces provided, write T if the statement is true; write F if the statement is false.

_____ 11. Adjudication of insanity generally has the same effect as death in terminating an offer.

_____ 12. The possibility that a contract *can* be performed within one year is enough to remove it from operation of the statute of frauds.

_____ 13. Written agreements to answer for the debt or default of another are unenforceable if the promisor's purpose was to become secondarily liable.

_____ 14. When an agreement made in consideration of marriage is put in writing, the consideration must be stated on the face of the document.

_____ 15. As far as contract law is concerned, only sales and contracts to sell goods are governed by the Uniform Commercial Code; transactions involving realty, services, or the sale of intangibles are excluded from coverage.

_____ 16. A threat of civil action constitutes duress if the person receiving the threat believes that the suit will be successful.

_____ 17. The mutual promises in a bilateral contract need not be express; one of the promises could be implied from the surrounding circumstances.

_____ 18. If the objectives of an agreement are illegal, the agreement is illegal—even though the parties were not aware of the illegality when they arrived at their agreement.

_____ 19. A bilateral contract between an adult and a minor is voidable by either party.

_____ 20. Once an express warranty is created, it can be disclaimed only in writing.

Multiple-Choice Questions

In the spaces provided, write the letter of the response that best completes each statement.

_____ 21. Which of the following does _not_ terminate an offer?
   a. Rejection of the offer
   b. Death of either party
   c. Counteroffer by offeree
   d. Request for additional terms by offeree

_____ 22. An offer to enter into a unilateral contract calls for an acceptance in the form of
   a. an express promise to perform an act.
   b. an implied promise to perform an act.
   c. actual performance of an act.
   d. silence or inaction.

_____ 23. If a contract is induced by innocent misrepresentation, the deceived party
   a. has the right of rescission.
   b. waives the right of rescission.
   c. cannot seek restitution.
   d. cannot sue for breach of contract.

_____ 24. Which of the following is *not* a requirement of an enforceable contract?
   a. Genuine assent of parties
   b. Equal consideration
   c. Competent parties
   d. Legality of agreement

_____ 25. An agreement to answer for the debt of another need *not* be in writing if the promisor intended to
   a. become primarily liable.
   b. become secondarily liable.
   c. benefit the original debtor.
   d. apply the leading object rule.

_____ 26. Any attempt to disclaim an express warranty is
   a. fraudulent.
   b. rescission.
   c. disaffirmance of contract.
   d. void.

_____ 27. Disaffirmance of contract by a minor may be made
   a. only in writing.
   b. by any expression of an intention to repudiate the contract.
   c. only when the minor reaches majority.
   d. even if the contract is wholly executed.

_____ 28. On acceptance, the terms of the offer become
   a. an invitation to negotiate.
   b. bilateral.
   c. a solicitation of an offer.
   d. the terms of the contract.

_____ 29. When a person is entitled to judicial relief in case of breach of contract by the other party, the contract is
   a. valid.
   b. void.
   c. voidable.
   d. unilateral.

_____ 30. Which of the following contracts is not governed by the statute of frauds?
   a. Agreement made in consideration of marriage
   b. Agreement for the sale of an interest in real property
   c. Agreement to disclaim an express warranty
   d. Agreement to answer for the debt or default of another

Completion Questions

Summarize Chapter VIII by filling in the blanks to complete the following statements.

31. A _____ is a legally enforceable agreement between
    _____ parties, based on
    genuine _____ of the parties, supported by
    _____, and does not contravene principles of
    _____.

32. A _____ contract is a binding and enforceable
    agreement, with all the necessary contractual requirements being
    present. A _____ contract has no legal effect
    whatsoever. A _____ contract comes into existence
    when one or more people can elect to avoid an obligation created by
    the contract.

33. If both parties to a contract make promises, the contract is
    _____. If only one party makes a promise, the
    contract is _____.

34. The usual manner in which the parties manifest assent in the
    formation of a contract is by one party making an
    _____ and the other party indicating
    _____.

35. Defenses against the enforceability of a contract include
    (a) _____, or any unlawful constraint exercised on a

person to force consent; (b) _____ influence, which results when a dominant person unlawfully substitutes his or her will for that of the other party; (c) _____, or intentional acts of deception to gain an advantage over the other party; (d) _____ misrepresentation of a material fact; and (e) a _____ or ignorance about some matter that influences a person to enter into a contractual relation.

36. _____ is that which is bargained for and given in exchange for another's promise. This inducement can be a _____, an _____, or a _____.

37. Full contractual _____ is met when a person is of legal age without mental disability or incapacity. The principal classes of people given some degree of special protection on their contracts because of incapacity are _____, _____ people, and _____ people.

38. An agreement is _____ when either its formation or performance is criminal, tortious, or contrary to public policy.

39. Statutes that require certain contracts to be in writing are called *statutes of* _____. Six types of contracts are so governed: (a) an agreement by an executor or administrator to answer for the debt of the _____; (b) an agreement made in consideration of _____; (c) an agreement to answer for the debt or default of _____; (d) an agreement that cannot be performed in _____; (e) an agreement for the sale of an interest in _____ property; and (f) an agreement for the sale of _____ above a certain dollar amount.

IX

Property

REVIEW TOOLS

Chapter Overview

This chapter focuses on the distinctions between real and personal property, tangible and intangible property, and fixtures. Also discussed are the various classifications of property ownership and the myriad ways in which title to both real and personal property can be acquired. Finally, the law of bailments, or the temporary acquisition of property, is addressed.

Key Topics

Historical development
Property classifications
    Real or personal
    Tangible or intangible
    Fixtures
   Property ownership
    Severalty
    Concurrent
    Community property
  Title
Government regulation
  Zoning
  Eminent domain
  Taxation

COURT CASES

Far West Modular Home Sales, Inc. v. Proaps

The plaintiff contracted to sell a modular home to the defendants. The home was delivered in two sections, mounted and secured on a concrete foundation by bolts and nails, and connected to all utilities. After a price dispute arose, the plaintiff filed an action in replevin to recover the property. Following a jury-waived trial, the court found for the plaintiff.

On appeal, the appellate court in Oregon reversed, holding that the modular home constituted a fixture on real property. The court examined three factors: adaptation (conceded by the plaintiff), annexation, and intent, and concluded that annexation and intent were established by the securing of the home to the foundation, the connection to all utilities, and the fact that it would cost $4,700 to remove the home and restore the land.

Penn Central Transportation Company v. New York City

In 1967, Grand Central Terminal in New York City was designated a landmark. In an effort to increase its income, the owner of the terminal, Penn Central, entered into a contract to have a multistory office building constructed above the building, a plan that required the approval of the Landmarks Preservation Commission. Penn Central's application for approval was denied by the commission.

Penn Central then brought suit, claiming that the Landmarks Preservation Law had resulted in a "taking" of their property without just compensation in violation of the U.S. Constitution. The trial court held for Penn Central. The New York Supreme Court, Appellate Division, reversed, and the New York Court of Appeals (the highest state court) affirmed.

The U.S. Supreme Court held that the law did not constitute a "taking," reasoning that the restrictions imposed were substantially related to the promotion of the general welfare, were not discriminatorily applied, and permitted Penn Central to continue utilizing the terminal so as to obtain a reasonable return on its investment.

Feeley v. Borough of Ridley Park

In an equity action brought by the Borough of Ridley Park, the appellant's home was held to be a public nuisance as a result of noxious odors arising from the unsanitary maintenance of approximately eighteen cats. After the appellant failed to comply fully with a preliminary injunction, a chancellor issued a final order requiring her to keep only four cats, to have them examined by a veterinarian, and to have her home professionally cleaned and deodorized.

In agreeing with the chancellor, the appellate court ruled that the appellant's use of her home was unreasonable and unwarranted and constituted a public nuisance. The court further held that the borough had the authority to abate the nuisance in the manner prescribed by the chancellor.

Sherwood Estates Homes Association, Inc. v. McConnell

In this action, the Sherwood Estates Homes Association brought suit to compel the removal of a dog pen erected by the appellant in his back yard pursuant to a restriction, known to the appellant, requiring prior approval for construction of such a pen.

The trial court concluded that the dog pen was a "structure" within the meaning of the restriction at issue and ordered its removal. The appellate court affirmed, reasoning that the intent of the declaration of restrictions was to maintain a harmonious residential area and to safeguard against the effects of any structures on the surrounding area and dwellings.

Favorite v. Miller

The defendant located and excavated a fragment of a statue of King George III from the plaintiff's property without the plaintiff's knowledge or permission and then sold the fragment to the Museum of the City of New York. The plaintiff sued to recover the fragment.

The trial court found for the plaintiff, concluding that the statue had been "mislaid" by the British Loyalists and, thus, rightly belonged to the landowner. On appeal, the Supreme Court of Connecticut affirmed but on different grounds. It ruled that the defendant's status as a trespasser, and the fact that excavation was necessary to recover the fragment, defeated any claim the defendant may have had as a "finder."

York v. Jones

The Yorks were participants in an *in vitro* fertilization program. When they joined the program, they signed a consent form that detailed the cryopreservation of any eggs (or prezygotes) in excess of five removed from Mrs. York's body.

During the procedure, six eggs were removed from Mrs. York, all were fertilized, and five were transferred to her uterus. The Yorks, who by that point had moved to California, requested that the sixth prezygote be transferred to an institution in California. The defendant refused, claiming that the consent form did not provide for such an interinstitutional transfer of a prezygote.

The court, in a case of first impression, concluded that the agreement created a bailor-bailee relationship that incorporated an absolute obligation to return the subject matter of the bailment to the bailor.

O'Brien v. O'Brien

Plaintiff-husband and defendant-wife were married in 1971. At the time, they were both private school teachers. The wife did not pursue her permanent certification in order to allow her husband to finish college and attend medical school. During medical school, the wife contributed all her earnings to their joint expenses. Two months after receiving his medical license, the husband filed for divorce.

The issue before the court was whether the husband's medical license constituted marital property subject to equitable distribution under New York law. After conflicting holdings in the lower courts, the New York Court of Appeals conclusively determined that the license did constitute marital property and could, therefore, be distributed at the dissolution of the marriage.

REVIEW QUESTIONS

Key Terms

In the spaces provided, write the letter of each term described. Not all terms are described.

a. eminent domain
b. personal property
c. private nuisance
d. title
e. fee simple
f. bailee

g. replevin
h. real property
i. easement
j. fixture
k. bailment
l. public nuisance

_____ 1. Ownership rights in property

_____ 2. An action to have personal property returned to its original possessor

_____ 3. The right of government to take private property for a public purpose

_____ 4. Exists when the use of land poses a generalized threat to the public

_____ 5. Maximum ownership rights to land permissible by law

_____ 6. A tort that requires proof of injury distinct from that suffered by the general public

_____ 7. Movable physical objects, intangible rights arising out of ownership of such objects, and intangible property

_____ 8. The person to whom personal property is delivered without title being conveyed

_____ 9. Immovable property

_____ 10. The transfer of possession of personal property on a nonpermanent basis

True-False Questions

In the spaces provided, write T if the statement is true; write F if the statement is false.

_____ 11. When a tenant in common dies, the rights of the deceased are inherited by the remaining tenant or tenants.

_____ 12. Tenancy by the entirety can exist only between legally married husbands and wives.

_____ 13. The police power of a state is derived from the U.S. Constitution.

_____ 14. No more than one person can have personal rights to the same object.

_____ 15. Concurrent ownership includes joint tenancy, tenancy in common, and tenancy by the entirety.

_____ 16. The Sixth Amendment provides that just compensation be paid when the government exercises eminent domain.

_____ 17. Life estates cannot be passed on to heirs.

_____ 18. Easements are generally enforceable whether in writing or not.

_____ 19. A bailment and a sale are similar in that title accompanies the object being delivered or sold.

_____ 20. To obtain property by adverse possession, the adverse possessor must live on the property with the knowledge of the previous owner.

Multiple-Choice Questions

In the spaces provided, write the letter of the response that best completes each statement.

_____ 21. Who has the primary responsibility for defining and limiting the exercise of private property rights?
a. Federal government
b. State courts
c. Federal courts
d. State government

_____ 22. Personal property does *not* include
a. copyrights.
b. stocks.
c. built-in dishwashers.
d. money.

_____ 23. The exceptions to the rules of title that purchasers of goods sold by merchants take title even if the goods were obtained illegally were created due to
a. the Uniform Commercial code.
b. public policy.
c. contract law.
d. severalty ownership.

_____ 24. If A allows B to use a private road on A's property, B has been granted
a. an easement.
b. a covenant.
c. a license.
d. a leasehold.

_____ 25. Which of the following is *not* a requirement for a covenant to run with the land?
a. Privity of estate
b. Grantor and grantee must issue personal guarantees.
c. The covenant must touch and concern the land.
d. Grantor and grantee must have intended that the restrictions follow the land.

_____ 26. To obtain title by adverse possession, the adverse possessor must
a. possess the land openly and notoriously.
b. take actual possession of the land in hostility.
c. reside on the property continuously for a minimum of one year.
d. both a and b.

_____ 27. A person who delivers personal property without conveying title thereto is a
a. bailee.
b. grantor.
c. grantee.
d. bailor.

_____ 28. Bailments are often created by
a. contract.
b. promise.
c. covenant.
d. license.

_____ 29. When property is divided among remaining survivors, but not through the laws of testacy or intestacy, the property was owned as
a. severalty ownership.
b. tenancy by the entirety.
c. joint tenants.
d. tenants in common.

_____ 30. A bailment exists when
a. a person barters legal services for housecleaning.
b. a person leaves clothes at a dry cleaner's.
c. a person sells a lawnmower.
d. a person allows his swing set to be used on a regular basis by the neighbor's child.

Completion Questions

Summarize Chapter IX by filling in the blanks to complete the following statements.

31. Real property is distinguishable from personal property in that real property is _____ . Personal property is generally comprised of _____ , _____ , and _____ .

32. The _____ of each state governs _____ , but the _____ primarily controls _____ and _____ .

33. _____ defines and limits the exercise of private property rights through its _____ .

34. The three forms of property ownership are (1) _____ , (2) _____ , and (3) _____ .

35. A person who has an _____ for the duration of his or her life has a _____ in land. A person who leases real property has a _____ in land entitled a _____ .

36. A _____ is a _____ grant of authority to do something in particular on another person's land. Licenses may be _____ and can usually be _____ .

37. Bailments involve _____ and _____ . The most common type of bailment is the _____ . There is no _____ or _____ involved.

38. Eight ways to acquire title to personal property are

(1) _____ , (2) _____ ,

(3) _____ , (4) _____ ,

(5) _____ , (6) _____ ,

(7) _____ , and (8) _____ .

39. An adverse possessor must take _____ of the land, the possession must be _____ and _____ , and it must continue for a _____ period of time.

40. The _____ provides notice of claims against real property to prospective purchasers of land. Each instrument is recorded at the _____ . _____ , _____ , _____ , and _____ are among the documents that are recorded.

X

The Law
of Torts

REVIEW TOOLS

Chapter Overview

Chapter X discusses the law of torts, which seeks to reimburse members of society who suffer losses because of the dangerous or unreasonable conduct of others. Since social injustices are the primary targets of tort law, the law changes to meet the needs and trends of society. New torts are created when a person's rights are violated but the law has not yet provided a remedy.

The chapter examines the various intentional torts, the principles of negligence, and the theories of strict liability, including product liability.

Key Topics

Historical view
Functions of tort law
Intentional torts
    Assault
    Battery
    Conversion
    Trespass
    Malicious prosecution
    False imprisonment
    Defamation
    Interference with contract relations
    Infliction of mental distress

            Invasion of privacy
Negligence
      Malpractice
      Duty of care
      Liability rules for specialized activities
      Proximate cause
      Contributory negligence and assumption of risk
      Comparative negligence
      Product liability
      Imputed negligence
      No-fault liability statutes
Strict liability
      Abnormally dangerous activities
      Product liability
         Breach of warranty
         Negligence
         Strict liability

COURT CASES

Estate of Berthiaume v. Pratt, M.D.

The plaintiff, as administratrix of her husband's estate, brought an action for invasion of privacy and for assault and battery based on photographs taken of her dying husband by his physician despite the husband's physical indications that he did not want to be photographed. In taking the pictures, the physician lifted the decedent's head, which accounts for the assault and battery charge. The husband died later that day.

    The lower court granted the physician's motion for a directed verdict. The Supreme Judicial Court of Maine reversed, reasoning that the jury could have found that the decedent's right to privacy had been invaded, and that assault and battery had occurred when the patient was touched without his consent for purposes other than treatment. A new trial was ordered.

Ivancic v. Olmstead

The plaintiff was injured during a windstorm by an overhanging limb from a tree on his parents' neighbors' property. He brought suit for negligence and trespass. The trial court submitted the case to a jury on a negligence theory, and the jury awarded the plaintiff money damages. Both parties sought to set aside the verdict, and a new trial was held. On cross-appeals, the New York appellate court reversed and dismissed the complaint on the ground that the defendant did not have constructive notice of a defect in the tree and, thus, no liability for negligence could ensue.

The Court of Appeals of New York (the highest state court) agreed with the appellate division's conclusion that the plaintiff had failed to establish a prima facie case of negligence. The court also determined that overhanging tree branches are not an intentional invasion of property and do not, therefore, constitute a trespass.

Hainz v. Shopko Stores, Inc.

The plaintiffs, two men, were detained for approximately fifteen minutes at a Shopko Store because store employees believed that price tags had been switched on hunting arrows. After the plaintiffs were acquitted of criminal shoplifting charges, they brought suit against Shopko for false imprisonment. Shopko claimed immunity for its employees' actions under the Wisconsin shoplifting statute.

The trial court rejected the defendant's claim and the case was submitted to a jury, which returned a verdict for the plaintiffs that included compensatory and punitive damages. Shopko appealed, and the state appellate court reversed and ordered the trial court to direct a verdict in the defendant's favor. The court ruled, as a matter of law, that merchants do not have an affirmative duty to investigate a customer's version of the underlying facts and concluded that the plaintiffs' detention was conducted "in a reasonable manner." The defendant, therefore, was entitled to immunity from civil liability under the state statute.

Carson v. Here's Johnny Portable Toilets, Inc.

Johnny Carson brought an action in U.S. District Court against a Michigan corporation operating under the name of "Here's Johnny Portable Toilets, Inc." Carson sought damages and an injunction preventing the defendant from using "Here's Johnny," claiming invasion of the rights of privacy and publicity. The court determined that the "likelihood of confusion" standard had not been met and, thus, dismissed the complaint.

The U.S. Court of Appeals reversed, agreeing that the trial court was correct in ruling that Carson's right of privacy had not been infringed but concluding that a celebrity's legal right of publicity is violated when an appropriation of that person's identity occurs, even if his or her name and/or likeness is not used.

Gilhooley v. Star Market Co., Inc.

The plaintiff was injured when he slipped on a green pepper in the produce department of a grocery store owned and operated by the Star Market Company. He alleged that his injury was the result of the defendant's negligence, and the matter was tried by a jury. The court entered judgment for the defendant after the jury returned a verdict in favor of the store. The plaintiff appealed, claiming that the trial judge had refused to give a requested instruction with respect to the store's duty to display and market its peppers. The intermediate court of appeals, however, disagreed with the plaintiff and affirmed the trial court's judgment. The plaintiff again appealed, this time to the state supreme court. That court affirmed the decision of the lower courts. The evidence indicated that the store had complied with industry practices in displaying its merchandise and had established adequate monitoring procedures. The state supreme court concluded that the trial judge's jury instructions were correct.

Weirum v. RKO General, Inc.

An action was brought for the wrongful death of the plaintiff's decedent, who was killed when his automobile was forced off a highway by a person responding to the defendant radio station's contest rewarding the first contestant to locate a peripatetic disc jockey.

The jury returned a verdict against the defendant, who appealed. The Supreme Court of California held that the radio station was liable because it was foreseeable that the broadcaster's youthful listeners would race to arrive first at the desired destination and in their haste would disregard highway safety.

Wright v. Webb

Joann Webb was attacked in the parking lot of a motel owned by the Wrights. After the attack, Webb filed suit for negligence, alleging that the Wrights failed to provide adequate security to protect business invitees from "foreseeable criminal attack." A jury returned a verdict in her favor.

The Wrights appealed, and the Supreme Court of Virginia reversed, holding that a motel has an affirmative duty to protect business invitees only when it knows that criminal assaults are occurring or that such attacks are imminently probable. The court entered final judgment for the defendant.

Anglin v. Florida Department of Transportation

The Anglins filed suit against the Florida Department of Transportation and a railroad company, alleging negligence in designing and maintaining a road and railway tracks. The Anglins' pickup truck had stalled in a six-inch accumulation of water on a highway, and Mrs. Anglin was seriously injured when another vehicle, attempting to provide assistance, collided with the truck. The trial court granted the defendants' motion for summary judgment, holding that the collision and the plaintiffs' actions in trying to push-start their truck were independent, intervening causes that were unforeseeable to the defendants.

The appellate court reversed. It ruled that the plaintiffs' actions were not an independent, intervening cause of the accident since the pool of water on the roadway initially created the situation. The court further held that although the good samaritan's negligent conduct constituted an intervening cause, it was for a jury to decide whether his actions were reasonably foreseeable and, thus, could be attributed to the defendants' negligence.

Stein v. Langer

After experiencing mechanical difficulties, Stein, a truck driver, pulled onto the shoulder of a highway. Because the shoulder was narrow, the truck remained partially on the road. A passing friend, Cooper, pulled over and parked his truck facing Stein's truck in order to provide a jump-start. To conserve his battery, Stein turned his lights off; Cooper's lights and flashers were on.

The defendant, Langer, hit Stein's truck with his car, pushing Stein's truck into the front of Cooper's truck. Stein was standing between the trucks at the time and was injured. He brought suit, and the jury returned a verdict finding Langer 55 percent negligent and Stein 45 percent negligent. No fault was attributed to Cooper. The court entered judgment against Langer, reducing the damage award by 45 percent. The plaintiff appealed, alleging that "the jury erred in assessing fault and in awarding him inadequate damages." The court of appeals affirmed the jury's allocation of fault.

Laaperi v. Sears, Roebuck & Co., Inc.

Laaperi, as administrator of the estate of his three sons and on behalf of his injured daughter, brought suit against Sears, Roebuck and another defendant for negligent design and manufacturing, breach of warranty, and negligent failure to warn about the inherent dangers of a smoke detector purchased from Sears. The smoke detector failed to sound an alarm when an electrical fire, caused by a short circuit, occurred in the Laaperi home. The trial court directed verdicts in favor of the defendants on all claims except for the negligent failure to warn. On that claim, the jury awarded slightly more than one million dollars for the deceased sons' actions and $750,000 for the injured daughter's claim. The court denied the defendants' motions for a directed verdict and judgment notwithstanding the verdict.

The defendants appealed to the U.S. Court of Appeals for the First Circuit. Based on Massachusetts law, the court affirmed the lower court's judgment as to the actions brought on behalf of the three sons, concluding that the issue of whether a warning was needed that an electrical fire would incapacitate an electric-powered smoke detector was a jury question. The court, however, vacated the daughter's award and remanded for a new trial on damages since the law provided that she could receive compensation only for personal injuries suffered, not for grief incident to the loss of her three brothers.

Westberry v. Blackwell

While walking toward the defendants' house, the plaintiff received a superficial bite by the defendants' dog. After the plaintiff's son informed the defendants that the dog had tried to bite him, the plaintiff was again bitten by the dog, requiring stitches. The plaintiff sued under the theories of strict liability and negligence. The trial court granted a judgment of involuntary nonsuit on both causes of action.

The Supreme Court of Oregon reversed, holding that a jury could have reasonably concluded that the defendants knew or had reason to know of the dog's tendency to bite, which would result in the defendants being strictly liable. The court further concluded that it was for a jury to determine whether the defendants were negligent in not confining their dog.

Leichtamer v. American Motors Corp.

The Leichtamers were passengers in a jeep that turned upside down, resulting in serious injuries to them and death to the driver and his wife. The Leichtamers brought suit, claiming that the collapse of the roll bar support on the jeep was causally related to their injuries. After a trial, the jury found for the Leichtamers, and the defendants appealed.

The appellants argued that strict liability principles should not apply in a design defect case involving a "second collision" (when the alleged defect enhances the injuries).

The court disagreed and stated that strict liability in tort has been applied to design defect "second collision" cases. Where plaintiffs can demonstrate sufficient evidence that an unreasonably dangerous product design proximately caused or enhanced their injuries in the course of foreseeable use, instructions on strict liability are proper.

REVIEW QUESTIONS

Key Terms

In the spaces provided, write the letter of each term described. Not all terms are described.

a. invitee
b. vicarious liability
c. assumption of risk

d. libel
e. battery
f. comparative negligence

g. assault
h. negligence
i. proximate cause

j. strict liability
k. slander
l. conversion

_____ 1. Defamation expressed by print, writing, signs, or pictures

_____ 2. The failure to exercise reasonable care demanded by the particular circumstances existing at the time of the act

_____ 3. An unpermitted, unprivileged, intentional contact with another's person

_____ 4. Imputed negligence arising by reason of some relationship existing between two parties

_____ 5. Any unauthorized act that deprives an owner of the possession of tangible personal property

_____ 6. Exists when the plaintiff expressly or impliedly consents to relieve the defendant of liability

_____ 7. Defamation expressed by spoken words in the presence of someone other than the party defamed

_____ 8. An act—other than the utterance of words—that puts another in apprehension of immediate and harmful contact

_____ 9. A reasonable connection between the negligent act of the defendant and the damage suffered by the plaintiff

_____ 10. Imposes legal responsibilities for injuries caused by certain dangerous instrumentalities without proof of lack of due care

True-False Questions

In the spaces provided, write T if the statement is true; write F if the statement is false.

_____ 11. Individuals are not all held to the same objective standards regarding negligence.

_____ 12. Generally, truth of the statement is a complete defense in suits for both defamation and invasion of privacy.

_____ 13. Prosecutors of criminal cases are absolutely immune from malicious prosecution suits, even if it is shown that they acted in bad faith.

_____ 14. The motive or purpose of a party who interferes with contract relations is an important factor in determining liability.

_____ 15. Assumption of risk must be expressed; it cannot be implied.

_____ 16. Battery includes physical contact that is merely offensive to the particular plaintiff.

_____ 17. Today, the infliction of mental distress is generally considered to be an intentional tort that should serve as a basis of recovery apart from any other tort.

_____ 18. Generally, the motives of the defendant are unimportant in suits for invasion of privacy.

_____ 19. When a person buys a product from a merchant the law considers the seller to have implicitly warranted its fitness.

_____ 20. Generally, words alone constitute an assault as long as they place the hearer in a state of apprehension.

Multiple-Choice Questions

In the spaces provided, write the letter of the response that best completes each statement.

_____ 21. There is no negligence and no liability if the defendant
   a. was imprudent but had no intent to inflict injury.
   b. could not reasonably foresee any injury as a result of the conduct.
   c. suffered a loss comparable to the plaintiff's as a result of the conduct.
   d. is a child, a doctor, or a lawyer.

_____ 22. The liability of an employer for the torts committed by employees within the scope of their employment is an example of
   a. assumption of risk.
   b. contributory negligence.
   c. wanton misconduct.
   d. imputed negligence.

_____ 23. In suits involving a landowner's negligence, the courts give the greatest protection to
   a. social guests.
   b. licensees.
   c. invitees.
   d. trespassers.

_____ 24. Strict liability in tort has been applied throughout the United States to
   a. product liability cases.
   b. assault and battery cases.
   c. malicious prosecution cases.
   d. libel and slander cases.

_____ 25. Generally, truth of the statement is a complete defense in
   a. invasion-of-privacy cases.
   b. libel and slander cases.
   c. both a and b.
   d. neither a nor b.

_____ 26. Which of the following is *not* a necessary element for a cause of action in negligence?
   a. Reasonable evidence of intent to inflict injury
   b. A duty or standard of care recognized by law
   c. A breach of the duty of failure to exercise the requisite care
   d. The occurrence of harm proximately caused by the breach of duty

_____ 27. A party who refuses to return goods to their owner is liable for
   a. breach of contract.
   b. conversion.
   c. defamation.
   d. wanton misconduct.

_____ 28. Two defenses in negligence cases are
   a. contributory negligence and imputed negligence.
   b. assumption of risk and contributory negligence.
   c. vicarious liability and comparative negligence.
   d. malicious prosecution and conversion.

_____ 29. In tort law, a reasonable connection between the defendant's negligent act and the damage suffered by the plaintiff is called
   a. causation in fact.
   b. causation *in extremis*.
   c. probable cause.
   d. proximate cause.

_____ 30. The duty of exercising care to protect another may be imposed by
   a. legislative acts.
   b. judicial decisions.
   c. both a and b.
   d. neither a nor b.

Completion Questions

Summarize Chapter X by filling in the blanks to complete the following statements.

31. The essential elements for recovery for a tortious act are the existence of a _____ and _____ that breaches that _____ , producing an _____ .

32. _____ is the failure to exercise the degree of _____ demanded by the particular circumstances existing at the time of the act. If the defendant could not _____ foresee any injury as the result of conduct, there is no _____ and no _____ .

33. The duty of exercising care to protect another may be imposed by _____ acts or by _____ decisions. As a general rule, the law does not impose the duty to aid or protect another, although a duty is imposed where there is a special _____ between the parties (as between parent and child or employer and employee).

34. The ordinary principles of negligence do not always govern the liability of a land occupier or possessor who owes a lesser duty to those who visit the premises. This reflects the common law classification of the visitors as _____ , _____ , or _____ . An _____ is given the greatest protection by the courts.

35. For the plaintiff to support a cause of action in negligence, there must be a _____ connection between the negligent act of the defendant and the damage suffered by the plaintiff. In tort law, this connection is called _____ cause.

36. _____ negligence is a defense that prevents recovery for negligence if the injured person by his own negligence proximately contributed to the injury. The defense of _____ of _____ exists when the plaintiff actually had knowledge of the _____ and made the free choice to accept it.

37. _____ negligence results when one person (_____) acts for or represents another (_____) by the latter's authority and to accomplish his ends. One is not accountable for the negligent act of an independent _____ .

38. Unlike negligence, which is based on failure to use reasonable care, _____ torts are based on willful misconduct. The law finds _____ where a reasonable person would believe that a particular result was substantially certain to follow.

39. A party who has become a public figure has waived the right of _____ , and society has a right to information of legitimate public interest. Nonetheless, civil liability for the intentional tort of _____ results from the act of injuring one's character, fame, or reputation by false and malicious statements.

40. _____ is defamation expressed by print, writing, signs, or pictures. _____ involves words spoken in the presence of someone other than the person defamed.

41. _____ is an attempt to inflict injury on another person when there is opportunity of doing so. An unpermitted, unprivileged, intentional contact with another's person is defined as _____ . The party injured by such conduct may

bring both _____ and _____ actions, which are independent of each other.

42. Any unauthorized act that deprives an owner of possession of tangible personal property is _____ . An intentional tort also takes place when a noncontracting party or third person wrongfully interferes with _____ relations. The intentional tort of _____ includes every unauthorized entry on the land of another and any offense or transgression that damages another's personal property. The restraint of a person's liberty against the person's will and without authority is _____ imprisonment.

43. _____ liability imposes legal responsibilities for injuries caused by certain dangerous instrumentalities without proof of lack of due _____ . This theory of recovery has been applied to _____ liability cases.

XI

Administrative Law & Administrative Agencies

REVIEW TOOLS

Chapter Overview

Government regulation of businesses is primarily exercised through administrative agencies and administrative law. This chapter describes the means of creating administrative agencies, as well as the roles and limitations of the various agencies. Generally, the broad powers given to administrative agencies include investigations, rule making, and adjudicatory hearings. Procedural due process must be followed when executing these functions. The scope and timing of judicial review of administrative actions is also discussed. The chapter concludes with an introduction to some of the more important administrative agencies, such as the Occupational Safety and Health Administration and the Environmental Protection Agency.

Key Topics

The development of administrative agencies
Organization and classification
    The function of administrative agencies
Agency powers
    Rule-making power
    Investigative power
    Adjudicative power
Judicial review
    Timing of review

Recognition of administrative competence and scope of review
Regulation of businesses
    OSHA
    Federal Trade Commission and consumer protection legislation
Environmental Protection Agency
    Air pollution
    Water pollution and the Clean Water Act
    Pesticide control
    Hazardous wastes disposal
    Practical impact of regulations

COURT CASES

Askildson v. Commissioner of Public Safety

Askildson's driving privileges had been revoked as a result of numerous DWI offenses. In 1985, the commissioner of public safety reinstated the appellant's license conditioned on his total abstinence. One year later, Askildson's license was again revoked when he was found intoxicated in a restaurant. The appellant petitioned the trial court to reinstate his license, claiming that the commissioner had overstepped his powers and that no findings were made that his use of alcohol in a restaurant was a public safety hazard. The trial court denied the requested relief.

The Minnesota court of appeals affirmed the lower court and ruled that the commissioner had the authority to condition reinstatement of a driver's license upon total abstinence from alcohol. The court also held that the revocation of Askildson's license for drinking in a nondriving situation was neither arbitrary nor capricious.

Chip Steak Company v. Hardin

The plaintiffs brought an action for declaratory and injunctive relief with respect to an alleged practice of the Department of Agriculture in not approving labels declaring the presence of sorbic acid and sorbates in certain meat products. On cross-motions for summary judgment, the district court held that the secretary of agriculture has the power under the federal Meat Inspection Act to promulgate regulations prohibiting or restricting the use of food additives in meat products.

Dow Chemical Company v. United States

The Environmental Protection Agency (EPA) was denied permission to reinspect a large Dow Chemical plant. Without an administrative search warrant, the EPA hired an aerial photographer to fly above the plant and take photographs using a precision aerial mapping camera. Upon learning of the EPA's actions, Dow filed suit in U.S. District Court. Dow was awarded summary judgment and injunctive relief because the court concluded that the EPA's authority did not extend to taking aerial photographs and that the taking of such photographs constituted a violation of Dow's Fourth Amendment rights.

The EPA appealed to the U.S. Court of Appeals, which reversed. It ruled that Congress's delegation of general investigatory powers to the EPA was similar to that of law enforcement agencies and that the use of aerial photography as an investigative method was within the scope of the agency's authority.

Dow's petition for *certiorari* was granted by the U.S. Supreme Court. The Supreme Court affirmed the court of appeals, holding that the EPA did have statutory authority to conduct aerial observations and photography. The Court also held that a large industrial complex is more like an "open field" than "curtilage," and as such, the taking of aerial photographs within navigable airspace does not constitute a violation of the Fourth Amendment.

Arndt v. Department of Licensing and Regulation

The Department of Licensing and Regulation suspended the petitioner's contractor's license following an investigative hearing. Based on a building inspector's conclusion that Arndt's work was done poorly, which resulted in structural defects, the hearing examiner recommended a minimal fine. The board, however, suspended Arndt's license for six months and issued a substantial fine. Arndt appealed the circuit court's affirmance of the board's final order.

The Michigan appeals court held that the proceedings had been conducted in compliance with the state administrative procedures statute, that substantial evidence supported the suspension order, and that the sanctions imposed were neither arbitrary nor an abuse of discretion.

Whirlpool Corp. v. Marshall

Believing that their safety on the job was endangered, two employees of Whirlpool Corporation met with the plant maintenance supervisor. Dissatisfied with his response, the employees met with the plant safety director and requested the name of an OSHA representative. The next day, the employees refused to perform what they considered to be unsafe duties and, as a result, were directed to leave work without pay. They also received written reprimands.

The secretary of labor filed suit in U.S. District Court, claiming that Whirlpool's actions against the employees violated an Occupational Safety and Health Act provision prohibiting an employer from discriminating or discharging an employee who exercises a right afforded by the act. One such right, as set forth in a regulation promulgated by the secretary of labor, is to refuse to perform a job because of a reasonable fear of death or serious injury.

The district court held that the secretary's regulation was invalid because it was inconsistent with the act. On appeal, the Sixth Circuit Court of Appeals reversed. The U.S. Supreme Court upheld the circuit court's decision, concluding that pursuant to the "general duty" clause of the act, the secretary's regulation was within his statutory authority. The regulation furthered the objectives of the act by allowing employees a self-help mechanism if no reasonable alternative existed.

Southern Pines Associates v. United States

Pursuant to the Clean Water Act, the Environmental Protection Agency issued a violations notice to Southern Pines for discharging fill material into wetlands without a permit. Southern Pines filed a complaint and sought a temporary restraining order, claiming that the EPA lacked jurisdiction since the wetlands in question were not adjacent to any body of water. The federal district court dismissed the case on the ground of lack of subject matter jurisdiction.

The Fourth Circuit Court of Appeals affirmed, stating that Congress intended to preclude judicial review of compliance orders under the Clean Water Act. Since Southern Pines was not subjected to enforcement proceedings or penalties, the lack of notice did not constitute a due process violation.

REVIEW QUESTIONS

Key Terms

In the spaces provided, write the letter of each term described. Not all terms are described.

a. investigative power
b. finality
c. hearing
d. Administrative Due Process Act
e. enabling act
f. ripeness

g. exhaustion
h. separation of powers
i. Administrative Procedure Act
j. legislative rule
k. quasi-legislative power
l. adjudicatory hearing

_____ 1. Legislative authorization to create an administrative agency

_____ 2. That which is intended to, and does have, the force of law

_____ 3. Power conferred on practically all administrative agencies, without which they could not adequately perform their rule-making and adjudicatory functions

_____ 4. A quasi-judicial proceeding to determine the rights, duties, and obligations of a specific person or persons

_____ 5. The constitutional principle that the legislative, executive, and judicial functions of government should not exist in the same person or group of persons

_____ 6. Concerns whether or not an administrative position has crystallized and is, in fact, an institutional decision

_____ 7. Requires that general notice of proposed rule making by a federal agency be published in the _Federal Register_

_____ 8. An agency's power to make, alter, or repeal rules and regulations

_____ 9. Concerns whether or not the issues presented are appropriate for judicial resolution

_____ 10. The necessity to pursue a claim through all administrative channels before seeking judicial relief

True-False Questions

In the spaces provided, write T if the statement is true; write F if the statement is false.

_____ 11. Rule making is often referred to as the quasi-legislative function of administrative agencies.

_____ 12. The Administrative Procedure Act of 1946 requires general publication of a substantive rule in the _Federal Register_ not less than 30 days before its effective date.

_____ 13. Courts reverse an agency's finding of fact if procedural due process was lacking.

_____ 14. The exercise of adjudicatory power permits an administrative agency to deprive one of property without notice.

_____ 15. The broad powers of investigation, rule making, enforcement, and adjudication granted to administrative agencies go unchecked and often conflict with the constitutional principle of the separation of powers.

_____ 16. When a court holds an agency's original determination invalid, it usually makes its own final decision rather than remanding the case for further consideration by the agency.

_____ 17. Administrative agencies may be created by legislative or enabling acts, by executive orders authorized by statutes, or by constitutional provisions.

_____ 18. An agency that is making a binding determination that directly affects the legal rights of an individual must use procedures traditionally associated with the judicial process.

_____ 19. Courts increasingly see administrative agencies as adversaries in judicial review, and they often interfere with the administrative process.

_____ 20. The power to investigate is one of the functions that distinguishes agencies from courts.

Multiple-Choice Questions

In the spaces provided, write the letter of the response that best completes each statement.

_____ 21. An agency's power to make, alter, or repeal rules and regulations is a
a. quasi-legislative function.
b. quasi-judicial function.
c. quasi-legal function.
d. *de novo* function.

_____ 22. If an agency is acting fairly and reasonably with the grant of power constitutionally conferred,
a. no subsequent legislative act can impair it.
b. its administrative remedies cannot be exhausted.
c. its orders will not be reversed by courts.
d. its board members are listed in the *Federal Register*.

_____ 23. Although the creator of an agency, which is generally the legislature, retains the power to destroy it or alter the rules governing it, the judiciary retains the power of
a. repealing the agency's rules and regulations.
b. final review of the agency's determination.
c. investigating the agency's jurisdiction.
d. declaring enabling acts.

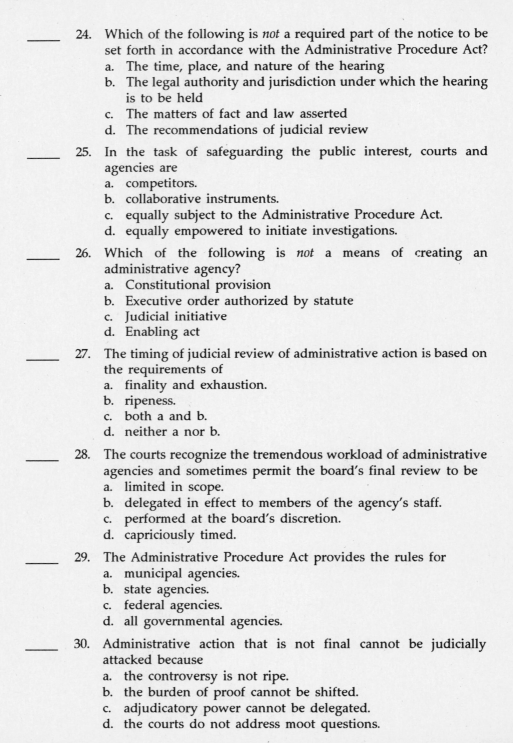

_____ 24. Which of the following is *not* a required part of the notice to be set forth in accordance with the Administrative Procedure Act?
a. The time, place, and nature of the hearing
b. The legal authority and jurisdiction under which the hearing is to be held
c. The matters of fact and law asserted
d. The recommendations of judicial review

_____ 25. In the task of safeguarding the public interest, courts and agencies are
a. competitors.
b. collaborative instruments.
c. equally subject to the Administrative Procedure Act.
d. equally empowered to initiate investigations.

_____ 26. Which of the following is *not* a means of creating an administrative agency?
a. Constitutional provision
b. Executive order authorized by statute
c. Judicial initiative
d. Enabling act

_____ 27. The timing of judicial review of administrative action is based on the requirements of
a. finality and exhaustion.
b. ripeness.
c. both a and b.
d. neither a nor b.

_____ 28. The courts recognize the tremendous workload of administrative agencies and sometimes permit the board's final review to be
a. limited in scope.
b. delegated in effect to members of the agency's staff.
c. performed at the board's discretion.
d. capriciously timed.

_____ 29. The Administrative Procedure Act provides the rules for
a. municipal agencies.
b. state agencies.
c. federal agencies.
d. all governmental agencies.

_____ 30. Administrative action that is not final cannot be judicially attacked because
a. the controversy is not ripe.
b. the burden of proof cannot be shifted.
c. adjudicatory power cannot be delegated.
d. the courts do not address moot questions.

Completion Questions

Summarize Chapter XI by filling in the blanks to complete the following statements.

31. Administrative agencies may be created by legislative or _____ acts, by executive _____ authorized by statutes, or by _____ provisions.

32. Agencies affect the rights of private parties and businesses by exercising powers of _____, _____, _____, and _____.

33. The power to _____ is one of the functions that distinguishes agencies from courts. Agencies cannot adequately perform their rule-making and _____ functions without access to facts.

34. Rule making is often referred to as the _____ legislative function of administrative agencies. To improve and strengthen the administrative process and preserve the basic limits on judicial review, Congress in 1946 passed the _____ Act.

35. The _____ function of administrative agencies involves the decision or determination of the rights, duties, and obligations of a specific person or persons. When making a binding determination that directly affects the legal rights of an individual, an agency must use the procedures that have traditionally been associated with the _____ process.

36. Before appealing to the courts for judicial review of an agency's actions, parties must _____ their administrative remedies by exploring every possible channel of relief. Administrative

action that is not final cannot be judicially attacked because the controversy is not _____ .

37. Courts do not reverse an agency's finding of fact unless (a) the action _____ the agency's granted power, (b) procedural _____ was lacking, or (c) there was lack of _____ evidence on the record as a whole to support its finding.

XII

Employment and Discrimination

REVIEW TOOLS

Chapter Overview

This chapter examines federal legislation enacted to protect against employment discrimination and the legal theories and defenses used when discrimination suits are brought. Title VII applies to employment discrimination on the basis of race, religion, sex, and national origin. The Age Discrimination in Employment Act provides protection from discrimination in the workplace to many individuals over the age of forty.

Also discussed is the National Labor Relations Board and the federal labor statutes that directly impact the rights of employees and employers, particularly with regard to unions and collective bargaining.

Key Topics

Employment discrimination
    History
    State legislation
Title VII
    Equal Employment Opportunity Commission
    Gender-based discrimination
    Religion
    Discrimination theories
    Employer defenses
    Affirmative action

COURT CASES

Jones v. Western Geophysical Co.

Jones, a black employee, was fired from his position at Western Geophysical Company after nearly five years of service. Jones contended, and the U.S. District Court agreed, that his termination was based on race and, thus, constituted a violation of Title VII and other federal statutes.

On appeal, the U.S. Court of Appeals for the Fifth Circuit affirmed, stating that Jones had presented a prima facie case and, despite the employer offering an allegedly legitimate, nondiscriminatory reason for the discharge, the evidence properly supported the district court's finding of intentional racial discrimination.

EEOC v. Red Baron Steak Houses

Amick was fired from her position as a waitress because she was pregnant. Sandra Spencer, an assistant manager, was terminated for refusing to fire Amick. In an action brought by the Equal Employment Opportunity Commission, the U.S. District Court held that the employer had committed both per se violations of Title VII and a prima facie case of employment discrimination with regard to Amick and retaliatory discharge with regard to Spencer.

The women were awarded damages, and the court issued a permanent injunction forbidding the defendant from violating Title VII in the future.

EEOC v. Ithaca Industries, Inc.

The EEOC brought suit on behalf of an employee who was terminated for refusing to work on Sunday, the employee's Sabbath, despite the employee having originally been told that Sunday work was voluntary. The U.S. District Court found for the company.

The U.S. Court of Appeals for the Fourth Circuit reversed, holding that the employer had violated section 701(j) of Title VII by failing to meet its burden of attempting to reasonably accommodate the religious needs of an employee. The court further reaffirmed that section 701(j) did not violate the First Amendment.

Sarni Original Dry Cleaners, Inc. v. Cooke

Cooke filed a complaint with the Massachusetts Commission Against Discrimination (MCAD), alleging that he was discharged from his job as a driver because of race following an incident in a primarily white neighborhood. The commission found for Cooke, and Sarni brought suit in superior court. Summary judgment was entered in favor of the employee, and Sarni appealed.

The Supreme Judicial Court affirmed and stated that Cooke had established a prima facie case of violation in a disparate treatment case. The defense of "bona fide occupational qualification" was not available to Sarni since it did not have a "factual basis for believing that all or substantially all [members of the excluded category] would be unable to perform safely and efficiently the duties of the job involved."

Lucas v. Dole

Plaintiff Lucas, a white woman, filed an action claiming reverse discrimination when a black woman with allegedly lesser qualifications received a promotion. The U.S. District Court dismissed the complaint, stating that the plaintiff had not established a prima facie case.

The U.S. Court of Appeals for the Fourth Circuit reversed, concluding that the plaintiff had demonstrated a prima facie case of disparate treatment under the test set forth in *McDonnell Douglas v. Green*. The plaintiff showed that she was a member of a protected group and that she was qualified for a job from which she was rejected. The court further stated that the plaintiff showed that race was a factor in the decision regarding promotion, a necessary requirement when the job remains open.

Stutts v. Freeman

The plaintiff was denied entry into an apprenticeship program for the position of heavy equipment operator based solely on low scores on a standardized written test. Both parties agree that the plaintiff was handicapped by virtue of having dyslexia. Results of nonwritten tests, which the employer unsuccessfully tried to obtain, demonstrated that plaintiff had the coordination, intelligence, and aptitude for the position.

The U.S. District Court granted summary judgment for the employer. The U.S. Court of Appeals for the Eleventh Circuit reversed and held that the employer's efforts to get the nonwritten test results did not constitute a "reasonable accommodation" of a handicapped person as required by the Rehabilitation Act of 1973.

EEOC v. El Paso Natural Gas Co.

At age sixty, corporate aircraft pilots of the employer were offered a nonflying position, if available, or were forced to retire. The EEOC brought suit on their behalf. In a jury-waived trial on liability only, the court found that the employer had satisfied its burden of demonstrating that the age-of-sixty rule is a bona fide occupational qualification in that it is impossible or highly impractical to deal with pilots over the age limit on an individualized basis. Judgment was entered for the defendants.

Chalk v. U.S. District Court Central District of California

After being diagnosed with AIDS, Chalk, the plaintiff, was barred from classroom teaching and reassigned to an administrative post. His motion for a preliminary injunction was denied by the U.S. District Court. Chalk then filed an emergency motion for an injunction pending appeal.

The U.S. Court of Appeals for the Ninth Circuit reversed. It held that the teacher had satisfied criteria for having an injunction issued by demonstrating a strong likelihood of success on the merits and irreparable injury. The court rejected the notion of unfounded fear as a reason for excluding a teacher from his classroom.

DeSantis v. Pacific Tel. & Tel. Co., Inc.

Three separate federal suits were brought by homosexual men and women on the basis of discrimination. The court consolidated the appeals after the U.S. District Court dismissed the complaints for failing to state a claim under Title VII. The U.S. Court of Appeals for the Ninth Circuit held that Title VII's prohibition against sex discrimination applies to gender-based discrimination only, not to sexual orientation, preference, or effeminacy. The judgments of the district court were affirmed.

Textile Workers v. Darlington Manufacturing Company

The defendant company operated a single textile mill in South Carolina. A majority of its stock was held by Deering Milliken, a company that operated seventeen textile manufacturers. In 1956, despite vigorous company resistance, a union won an election at Darlington Manufacturing. The company closed its operations as a result. The union filed charges, claiming violation of the National Labor Relations Act.

The National Labor Relations Board found that the plant closing was a violation of the act, and since Darlington was part of Deering Milliken, that company was found to have violated the act by closing part of its business for a discriminatory purpose.

The court of appeals denied enforcement, and the Supreme Court granted *certiorari*. It held that a company is permitted to close its entire operations for any reason, even if motivated by vindictiveness toward a union. The Supreme Court also held, however, that it is an unfair labor practice to close a portion of a business if the impetus is to "chill unionism" in the remaining plants and if that objective is reasonably foreseeable by the employer. The matter was remanded to the National Labor Relations Board for findings on purpose and effect.

Teamsters, Local 456 and J. R. Stevenson Corporation

The Stevenson company, a general contractor, entered into a collective bargaining agreement with Teamsters Local 456. Pursuant to the agreement, Stevenson employed a Teamster who performed virtually no work. That employee's job was assumed by another Teamster, despite Stevenson's assertion that it did not need the services of a Teamster. After Stevenson alerted the Teamsters Local that it did not want to enter into a new collective bargaining agreement and informed the nonworking employee that he was going to be discharged, the Teamsters picketed the job site. Stevenson agreed to sign a new agreement.

Stevenson brought an action, and the administrative law judge found that the Teamsters had violated section 8(b)(6) of the Taft-Hartley Act by forcing Stevenson to pay an employee who did not provide services or make a bona fide offer to perform services. The National Labor Relations Board agreed and ordered the Teamsters to "cease and desist from coercing employer to pay for unneeded services [and to] . . . [p]ost notice; reimburse employer for wages paid to, and reasonable expenses directly incurred in employment of, unneeded worker."

REVIEW QUESTIONS

Key Terms

In the spaces provided, write the letter of each term described. Not all terms are described.

a. Title VII
b. disparate treatment
c. BFOQ
d. employment-at-will
e. featherbedding
f. protected classes
g. front pay
h. affirmative action
i. disparate impact
j. ADEA
k. EEOC
l. secondary boycott

_____ 1. The doctrine permitting employers, in the absence of contracts stating otherwise, to discharge employees for any reason whatsoever

_____ 2. The dollar value of lost wages and benefits an unlawfully discharged employee would be receiving if rehired immediately

_____ 3. Legislation enacted to protect against employment discrimination

_____ 4. Treatment of different groups of employees differently

_____ 5. Federal legislation that protects many individuals against discrimination on the basis of age

_____ 6. Use of various means to expand the employment opportunities of women and minority males

_____ 7. Forcing an employer to pay for work that is not performed

_____ 8. Coercive action exerted to make customers refrain from patronizing an unfavored business

_____ 9. The agency created to handle all disputes arising under Title VII

_____ 10. Discrimination in employment practices regardless of intent

True-False Questions

In the spaces provided, write T if the statement is true; write F if the statement is false.

_____ 11. Under the ADEA, the plaintiff in a disparate treatment case has to prove that the employer intended to discriminate and that age was one factor.

_____ 12. All Title VII cases are tried by the court, not by a jury.

_____ 13. Title VII applies to public sector employees of fifteen or more persons only.

_____ 14. Under Title VII, religious organizations are permitted to discriminate in the appointment of clergy and in the operation of churches.

_____ 15. Wrongfully terminated employees can often recover in tort for infliction of emotional distress and breach of covenant.

_____ 16. Age is a protected class under Title VII legislation.

_____ 17. In disparate impact discrimination, only an employer's motive and intent are examined.

_____ 18. The employer in a disparate treatment case can defend by producing evidence of a reasonable business justification for use of a particular employment practice.

_____ 19. The bona fide occupational qualification is a defense in disparate treatment cases.

_____ 20. An employee can bring an action under section 1981 for sexual harassment on the job.

Multiple-Choice Questions

In the spaces provided, write the letter of the response that best completes each statement.

_____ 21. The ADEA does *not* provide protection to which of the following?
a. Federal judges
b. Teachers
c. Business executives receiving pensions of less than $44,000
d. Police officers

_____ 22. Occupational health and safety in the workplace and collective bargaining are protected by
a. administrative regulations.
b. state law.
c. federal law.
d. the National Labor Relations Board.

_____ 23. An employer found to be in violation of Title VII may be required to
a. rehire the person.
b. reinstate the person.
c. promote the person.
d. all of the above.

_____ 24. The U.S. Supreme Court first recognized sexual harassment as a form of sex discrimination under Title VII in
a. 1964.
b. 1980.
c. 1970.
d. 1988.

_____ 25. In a trial *de novo* following an EEOC decision, the U.S. District Court must
   a. defer to the EEOC's findings of fact.
   b. defer to the EEOC's conclusions of law.
   c. disregard the EEOC's findings of fact.
   d. accept testimony of prior witnesses.

_____ 26. The EEOC is *not* empowered to
   a. enact legislation.
   b. investigate employment situations.
   c. issue employment practice guidelines.
   d. require the implementation of affirmative action programs.

_____ 27. Title VII was originally created to protect against what type of discrimination?
   a. Religion
   b. Sex
   c. Age
   d. Race

_____ 28. The Americans with Disabilities Act will become effective on
   a. July 26, 1992.
   b. July 26, 1993.
   c. July 26, 1994.
   d. July 26, 1995.

_____ 29. In a disparate impact case, an employer may defend a discrimination claim by
   a. producing a legitimate, nondiscriminatory reason for its actions.
   b. producing evidence of a reasonable business justification for the challenged practice.
   c. producing evidence of a bona fide occupational qualification.
   d. producing evidence that any violative actions were unintentional.

_____ 30. Private sector employees bringing claims pursuant to the ADEA must
   a. try their cases to the court.
   b. try their cases to an administrative judge.
   c. try their cases to a jury.
   d. try their cases to the EEOC.

Completion Questions

Summarize Chapter II by filling in the blanks to complete the following statements.

31. Title VII cases are tried by the _____ because Congress did not incorporate the right to _____ in the statute.

32. Employers are required to treat _____ like any other medical condition pursuant to the _____.

33. Employers can be found liable for discrimination even if they lack discriminatory _____. This is called _____.

34. Once an employer produces evidence of a legitimate, nondiscriminatory reason for an employee's rejection, the _____ has the burden of _____ the trier of fact that the employer's reason is merely a _____ for discrimination.

35. Section 1981 protects against _____ when an employee is _____, but it does not apply to _____ that occurs while on the job.

36. The ADA will initially apply to most public and private employers with _____ employees. After 1994, it will apply to employers with _____ employees.

37. Quotas are permitted only where solely designed to _____ an employer's _____ of discrimination. Often, employers enter into _____ requiring affirmative action to avoid or end Title VII litigation.

38. The Wagner Act protects the right of a _____ to exist and asserts the rights of employees to _____ and _____ with a union without employer interference.

39. The NLRB oversees _____ and _____ the union elected to represent employees. It also _____ charges of _____ committed by either employers or unions.

40. An employer may not justify discrimination based on _____ for any reason. In some instances, an employer may discriminate on the basis of _____ , _____ , or _____ .

XIII

Antitrust

REVIEW TOOLS

Chapter Overview

This chapter examines antitrust legislation enacted to promote and protect free enterprise. Concerted action that unreasonably restrains trade is prohibited. The chapter explores what constitutes vertical and horizontal monopolies, as well as the standards used to determine whether specific conduct violates the Sherman, Clayton, Robinson-Patman, or Federal Trade Commission acts.

Key Topics

Historical overview
Antitrust legislation
    The Sherman Act
    The Clayton Act
    Tying contracts, interlocking directorates, mergers
    Forum shopping
    Exemptions from antitrust laws
    The Federal Trade Commission

COURT CASES

Continental T.V., Inc. v. GTE Sylvania, Inc.

GTE Sylvania enforced franchise agreements that prohibited the sale of its products from locations other than those specified. Continental, a franchised retailer, brought suit, claiming a violation of section 1 of the Sherman Act. The U.S. District Court, relying on *United States v. Arnold, Schwinn & Co.,* instructed the jury that vertical nonprice restraints constituted a *per se* violation of the act. The U.S. Court of Appeals reversed, concluding that geographical restrictions should be judged under the rule of reason.

On appeal, the Supreme Court expressly overruled the *per se* rule of *Schwinn* and held that vertical nonprice restrictions are to be examined under the rule of reason.

Palmer v. BRG of Georgia, Inc.

BRG and Bar/Bri (the trade name of a division of Harcourt Brace Jovanovich) were competitors in the law review course market from 1977 to 1979. In 1980, they entered into an agreement that gave BRG an exclusive license to market Bar/Bri materials in Georgia, but that also precluded BRG from marketing outside the state. Shortly thereafter, the price of BRG's course increased significantly.

Palmer, a law student, filed an action under the Sherman Act. The U.S. District Court granted summary judgment for BRG, and the U.S. Court of Appeals for the Eleventh Circuit affirmed. Both courts concluded that *per se* unlawful horizontal price fixing required an express agreement on price or price levels. The Supreme Court reversed, reaffirming that horizontal restrictions to minimize competition through the allocation of territories was *per se* illegal under the Sherman Act.

Business Electronics Corporation v. Sharp Electronics Corporation

Business Electronics was the exclusive retailer of Sharp's electronic calculators. After four years, a second retailer, Hartwell, was added to the territory. Business Electronics's prices remained lower. Hartwell threatened to close its dealership unless Sharp terminated Business Electronics's franchise.

Business Electronics sued, claiming a violation of the Sherman Act. A jury in the U.S. District Court found in its favor. The appeals court for the Fifth Circuit reversed. The Supreme Court affirmed the Fifth Circuit, concluding that termination of a "price-cutter," without an agreement on price with the remaining dealer, does not justify a *per se* violation. The Court held that the rule of reason applies to vertical restraints.

Best Brands Beverage, Inc. v. Falstaff Brewing Corp.

For several years, Best Brands operated under a master distributorship agreement with the defendant, Falstaff. In 1984, Falstaff dramatically increased its prices to Best Brands and simultaneously entered into a previously unheard of dual master agreement. Best Brands filed for a preliminary injunction in U.S. District Court.

The court granted the injunction, concluding that because Falstaff could not demonstrate a good faith justification for its actions, the price increase established a prima facie showing of discriminatory pricing in violation of the Robinson-Patman Act. The court determined that the increase, coupled with the loss of exclusivity, endangered Best Brands' survival in the business.

Boyertown Burial Casket Co. v. Amedco, Inc.

The defendant, Amedco, made a tender offer to purchase the outstanding stock of the plaintiff, Boyertown. The plaintiff sought a preliminary injunction, alleging that a violation of section 7 of the Clayton Act would occur if the defendant's offer were successful.

The U.S. District Court granted the injunction based on the plaintiff's showing of a reasonable probability that the effect of a takeover in the relevant market of burial caskets, and within the relevant geographical market of the United States and a particular area in California, would tend to create a monopoly or substantially lessen competition.

Illinois Brick Co. v. Illinois

Illinois Brick (the petitioner) manufactured and distributed concrete block. The block was then sold to contractors, who, in turn, submitted bids to general contractors. The general contractors then submitted bids to customers such as respondent, the state of Illinois. The state sued and sought treble damages pursuant to section 4 of the Clayton Act, alleging that the petitioners had combined and conspired to fix prices in violation of the Sherman Act.

The U.S. District Court granted partial summary judgment in favor of Illinois Brick, holding that as a matter of law only direct purchasers could sue for an alleged overcharge. The Court of Appeals reversed. The U.S. Supreme Court reversed the Court of Appeals and held that an indirect purchaser such as the state of Illinois could not show injury by establishing that the overcharge was "passed on." The Court stated that its previous holding in *Hanover Shoe, Inc. v. United Shoe Machinery Corp.*, that antitrust defendants could not introduce evidence that indirect purchasers were injured by an illegal overcharge, compelled the decision that it would be manifestly unjust to allow the offensive use of "pass-on" since a defensive use was forbidden.

F.T.C. v. Superior Court Trial Lawyers Association

A group of lawyers who represented indigent criminal defendants under the Criminal Justice Act refused to accept new cases until their hourly fees were increased. The Federal Trade Commission filed a complaint that alleged that the attorneys had conspired to fix prices and were engaged in a boycott in violation of section 5 of the Federal Trade Commission Act.

The FTC found that the lawyers' action was illegal *per se*. The Court of Appeals vacated that ruling and remanded for a hearing on whether the attorneys possessed "significant market power." The appellate court stated that although the lawyers' boycott unlawfully restrained competition, First Amendment principles protected their concerted conduct. Therefore, the *per se* rules should not be applied to the case.

The Supreme Court disagreed. It held that despite the social utility of procuring quality representation for indigent defendants, and although the price fixing and boycott resulted in reasonable fees, the action constituted an unlawful horizontal arrangement among competitors subject to the *per se* rules.

REVIEW QUESTIONS

Key Terms

In the spaces provided, write the letter of each term described. Not all terms are described.

a. rule of reason
b. horizontal restraint
c. interlocking directorate
d. Sherman Act
e. relevant market
f. Federal Trade Commission

g. Clayton Act
h. *per se* violation
i. merger
j. vertical restraint
k. tying contract
l. Robinson-Patman Act

_____ 1. A conclusive presumption that certain practices are patently unreasonable and, therefore, illegal

_____ 2. Exists when a commodity is sold only on the condition that the buyer purchase an additional product or service as well

_____ 3. Federal legislation that applies to all transactions in interstate commerce prohibiting mergers that tend to monopolize or that demonstrate a reasonable likelihood of substantially lessening competition

_____ 4. The standard for determining when a contract violates the Sherman Act

_____ 5. Anticompetitive business activities established by a group of companies or one company

_____ 6. Federal legislation that applies to all transactions affecting interstate commerce and was enacted to preserve and promote free enterprise within the U.S. economy

_____ 7. Anticompetitive business activities conducted by entities that control different levels of a business operation, such as a manufacturer and a dealer

_____ 8. Results when a person serves on the board of directors of competing corporations or substantial businesses that could compete against one another

_____ 9. Federal legislation that governs discriminatory pricing

_____ 10. The government agency empowered to investigate antitrust violations

True-False Questions

In the spaces provided, write T if the statement is true; write F if the statement is false.

_____ 11. The federal courts have generally held that state legislation stopping federally approved mergers is pre-empted by federal law.

_____ 12. A manufacturer who requires a distributor to sell its products at a fixed price is engaged in horizontal restraint of trade.

_____ 13. Plaintiffs are increasingly choosing to litigate antitrust actions in state courts rather than federal courts.

_____ 14. Vertical restraints are _per se_ illegal if they include an agreement on price or price levels.

_____ 15. The Clayton Act is broader in scope and power than the Sherman Act.

_____ 16. A manufacturer who requires a distributor to sell its product at a fixed price constitutes a vertical monopoly.

_____ 17. Section 2 of the Clayton Act expressly prohibits price discrimination in the purchasing and sale of goods.

_____ 18. Industries exempt from antitrust laws are typically more heavily regulated than those subject to such laws.

_____ 19. The FTC is empowered to bring civil and criminal actions against violators in both state and federal court.

_____ 20. Some of the practices deemed not to be illegal *per se* are agreements to control production, to allocate customers, and to divide markets.

Multiple-Choice Questions

In the spaces provided, write the letter of the response that best completes each statement.

_____ 21. The Sherman Act applies to all transactions affecting
   a. intrastate commerce.
   b. interstate commerce.
   c. mergers.
   d. monopolies.

_____ 22. Sanctions imposed on violators of the Sherman Act may not include
   a. individual fines.
   b. seizure of property transported across state lines.
   c. treble damages.
   d. imprisonment for a period of five years.

_____ 23. A practice held to be monopolistic under the Clayton Act is
   a. mergers.
   b. informal agreements.
   c. holding companies.
   d. all of the above.

_____ 24. In determining whether a violation under section 7 of the Clayton Act has occurred, the court must first decide whether
   a. discriminatory pricing has occurred.
   b. horizontal restraints have occurred.
   c. the defendant actively sought some power over a relevant market.
   d. vertical restraints have occurred.

_____ 25. The Clayton Act applies to all transactions
   a. in interstate commerce.
   b. in intrastate commerce.
   c. affecting intrastate commerce.
   d. affecting interstate commerce.

_____ 26. Which of the following practices is generally *not* considered illegal *per se*?
   a. Horizontal agreement to control production
   b. Vertical agreement to divide market
   c. Vertical agreement to fix prices
   d. Horizontal agreement to allocate customers

_____ 27. Major league baseball, utilities, and broadcasting are examples of
   a. industries exempt from antitrust laws.
   b. horizontal monopolies.
   c. vertical monopolies.
   d. self-regulated industries.

_____ 28. The prevention of price fixing, illegal boycotts, and illegal combinations of competitors is the responsibility of
   a. the FTC.
   b. the Sherman Act.
   c. the Clayton Act.
   d. the Robinson-Patman Act.

Completion Questions

Summarize Chapter XIII by filling in the blanks to complete the following statements.

29. Federal legislation comprising the core of antitrust laws includes the

   _____ , the _____ , and the

   _____ .

30. The Sherman Act was enacted to _____ and

   _____ free enterprise. It applies to all transactions

   that affect _____ .

31. One practice prohibited by section 2 of the _____ is

   price discrimination in the purchasing and sale of goods.

32. A person violates the principles of _____ when he

   or she serves on the board of directors of _____

companies or companies that _____ compete against one another.

33. A relevant market consists of a _____ market and a _____ market. The court must decide whether the power acquired is sufficient to control _____ or _____ in the market.

34. Four sanctions may be imposed on violators of the _____. First, a violator may receive a _____ and _____; second, an _____ may be granted; third, _____ damages may be imposed; and fourth, the government may _____ property transported across state lines.

35. A court terminates a discriminatory practice and awards damages for a Clayton Act violation unless a defendant can show that the _____ was due to _____ because of a _____ order, changing conditions affecting the _____ of the goods, or a _____ effort to meet the lower prices of competitors.

36. The _____ governs when a contract violates the Sherman Act. Only contracts that _____ trade are considered illegal.

37. The Federal Trade Commission is empowered to bring _____ actions against violators in _____ court.

38. In a _____ contract, a commodity is sold only on the condition that the buyer _____ another _____ or _____ as well. These activities are generally considered _____.

XIV

Alternative Dispute Resolution

REVIEW TOOLS

Chapter Overview

Litigation is time-consuming and expensive. Due to backlogs in the courts' calendars, civil matters often do not go to trial for years after a cause of action arises. As a result, parties are beginning to seek alternate methods of resolving disputes more expeditiously and less expensively. This chapter examines some of the different techniques of alternative dispute resolution (ADR), such as mediation, summary jury trials, and arbitration.

Key Topics

Overview of alternative dispute resolution
Court-annexed ADR
    Settlement conferences
    Summary jury trials
Voluntary ADR
Private trials
Jointly used ADR methods
    Mediation
    Mini-trials
    Voluntary arbitration
    Judicial enforcement of arbitration awards
    Court-annexed arbitration

COURT CASES

Pittsburgh Corning Corp. v. Bradley

The defendant, Pittsburgh Corning Corporation, asked the Supreme Court of Pennsylvania to exercise its plenary jurisdiction and issue a writ of prohibition precluding the implementation of a court rule that required parties involved in asbestos litigation to first participate in a bench trial (nonjury) with the subsequent right to demand a jury trial *de novo*. Pittsburgh Corning argued that the rule unconstitutionally violated the right to a trial by jury.

The court held that the need to dispose efficiently of the overwhelming number of asbestos cases, coupled with the right to demand a jury trial *de novo*, rendered the rule constitutional and necessary.

Kothe v. Smith

Smith was a defendant in a medical malpractice case. Three weeks prior to trial, a U.S. District Court judge held a pretrial conference and ordered the parties to conduct settlement negotiations. After confidentially learning that plaintiff would settle for $20,000, the judge suggested to the defendant that the matter be settled for between $20,000 and $30,000. The plaintiff's lowest demand, however, was $50,000. After one day of trial, the parties settled for $20,000 and the judge issued a penalty against defendant Smith.

Smith appealed, and the U.S. Court of Appeals for the Second Circuit vacated the judgment, holding that the judge's imposition of a penalty was an abuse of the sanction power under Rule 16(f) of the Federal Rules of Civil Procedure since courts are not permitted to coerce settlements.

Arabian American Oil Co. v. Scarfone

Two defendants filed a motion in U.S. District Court to excuse their participation in a summary jury trial, citing a Seventh Circuit Court of Appeals case that held that Rule 16 of the Federal Rules of Civil Procedure did not permit a court to compel parties to conduct summary trials. The district court in Florida stated that it found summary jury trials to be a "legitimate device . . . to provide litigants with the expeditious and just case resolution," and it denied the defendants' motion on the general issue of mandatory participation.

Rhea v. Massey-Ferguson, Inc.

The plaintiff, Rhea, brought suit against Massey-Ferguson for breach of implied warranty and negligent design of a tractor. Rhea originally sued in state court, but Massey-Ferguson removed the matter to federal court. The U.S. District Court, pursuant to its local rules, referred the case to mediation before trial. The proposed award was $100,000, which the plaintiff accepted and the defendant rejected. Thus, under the local rules, the defendant became liable for actual costs unless the verdict at trial was more than 10 percent below the $100,000 mediation evaluation. Because the plaintiff ultimately won $228,000 at trial, the court awarded him $5,400 in actual costs.

The defendant appealed, challenging the court's referral of the case to mediation as a violation of its Seventh Amendment right to a jury trial. The Sixth Circuit Court of Appeals affirmed the verdict and the assessment of costs. It concluded that the Constitution was not violated since a jury ultimately determined the disputed facts in the matter.

Garrity v. Lyle Stuart, Inc.

The New York Court of Appeals (the highest state court) vacated an arbitrator's award of punitive damages, holding that enforcement of such an award would violate public policy.

Gilling v. Eastern Airlines, Inc.

The plaintiffs were passengers aboard an Eastern Airlines plane from Miami to Martinique. They sued, alleging that they were wrongfully ejected from the flight during a stopover. The court referred the case to mandatory arbitration. Only the defendants' counsel attended the arbitration, at which she presented summaries of the defendants' position and read from a few passages of deposition testimony and answers to interrogatories. The arbitrator found for the plaintiffs, and the defendants moved for a trial *de novo*.

The plaintiffs opposed the motion, claiming that the defendants had failed to "participate meaningfully" in the arbitration. After the arbitrator issued findings of fact concluding that the defendants had not participated meaningfully in the arbitration, the court granted the motion for a trial *de novo* but imposed sanctions on the defendants in the nature of requiring Eastern Airlines to pay all costs and fees the plaintiffs incurred relating to both the arbitration and the opposition of the motion for a trial *de novo*.

REVIEW QUESTIONS

Key Terms

In the spaces provided, write the letter of each term described. Not all terms are described.

a. *de novo*
b. mini-trial
c. ADR

d. arbitration
e. bench trial
f. mediation

g. summary jury trial
h. court-annexed ADR
i. Seventh Amendment

j. private trial
k. settlement conference
l. arbitration award

_____ 1. The requirement of federal and state judicial systems that litigants participate in trial alternatives

_____ 2. A nonbinding technique conducted by a neutral party to help settle a case prior to trial

_____ 3. The presentation of issues before a panel, generally used to resolve business disputes

_____ 4. Guarantees the right to a jury trial

_____ 5. An abbreviated trial employing an advisory jury, resulting in a nonbinding verdict

_____ 6. A pretrial meeting with a judge to help resolve a dispute

_____ 7. A traditional jury trial

_____ 8. A trial conducted solely before a judge

_____ 9. A decision rendered by an arbitrator that becomes a final judgment unless challenged

_____ 10. An alternative dispute resolution technique conducted outside the judicial arena, involving the employment of judges and jurors

True-False Questions

In the spaces provided, write T if the statement is true; write F if the statement is false.

_____ 11. The Sixth Amendment to the Constitution guarantees the right to a jury trial.

_____ 12. Arbitration hearings are generally open to the public.

_____ 13. There is no right to a jury trial for litigants seeking equitable relief or for causes of actions unknown in common law.

_____ 14. Alternative dispute resolution participation is often a pretrial procedural requirement.

_____ 15. Although mediators evaluate each case to predict the outcome of a trial on the issues, they do not value settlements.

_____ 16. An arbitration award becomes a final judgment unless the parties reject it and demand a trial *de novo.*

_____ 17. Arbitration agreements are enforceable whether executed verbally or in writing.

_____ 18. Critics of a private court system fear that justice would be accessible only to the wealthy.

_____ 19. Court-annexed alternative dispute resolution is authorized primarily through local court rules.

_____ 20. Mini-trials are generally reserved for straightforward, uncomplicated cases, such as personal injury disputes.

Multiple-Choice Questions

In the spaces provided, write the letter of the response that best completes each statement.

_____ 21. In conducting a settlement conference, a judge has the authority to
   a. initiate the meeting.
   b. respond to a request for assistance from one or more of the parties.
   c. emphasize each side's strengths and weaknesses.
   d. all of the above.

_____ 22. The Judicial Improvements and Access to Justice Act provides that
   a. a trial *de novo* is available to all people.
   b. judges conduct settlement conferences in most cases.
   c. several federal courts operate experimental court-annexed arbitration programs for five years.
   d. several state courts operate experimental court-annexed arbitration programs for five years.

_____ 23. Which of the following is *not* a type of alternative dispute resolution?
   a. Summary jury trial
   b. Trial *de novo*
   c. Mediation
   d. Mini-trial

_____ 24. A summary jury trial involves
    a. a brief presentation of the case by each side.
    b. a nonbinding, advisory verdict.
    c. jury instructions by the presiding judge.
    d. all of the above.

_____ 25. Court-annexed arbitration results in a
    a. settlement.
    b. binding decision.
    c. nonbinding decision.
    d. mini-trial.

_____ 26. A person who selects arbitration waives the right embodied in which amendment to the U.S. Constitution?
    a. Fifth
    b. Seventh
    c. Sixth
    d. Eighth

_____ 27. An arbitrator derives authority from
    a. federal mediation statutes.
    b. the American Arbitration Association.
    c. voluntary agreement of the parties.
    d. contract law.

_____ 28. A formal hearing is *not* conducted in which of the following?
    a. Mediation
    b. Arbitration
    c. Private trial
    d. Summary jury trial

Completion Questions

Summarize Chapter XIV by filling in the blanks to complete the following statements.

29. Court-annexed arbitration is a _____ procedure that produces _____ decisions.

30. The most commonly used methods of alternative dispute resolution are _____, _____, _____, _____, _____, and _____.

31. The parties in a court-annexed mini-trial can _____ a judge's proposal, but may incur a _____ . A party who proceeds to trial but recovers less than the judge's proposal may be assessed a _____ .

32. A mediator generally (1) helps the parties _____ , (2) _____ the issues, (3) looks for _____ and _____ , and (4) prevents the parties from _____ .

33. Arbitrators do not follow _____ , nor are they obligated to prepare _____ .

34. A reviewing court does not review an arbitrator's _____ .

Answers to Chapter Review Questions

CHAPTER I

Key Terms

1.	j	5.	a	8.	h
2.	l	6.	c	9.	f
3.	d	7.	i	10.	k
4.	g				

True-False Questions

11.	T	15.	F	18.	F
12.	F	16.	T	19.	T
13.	F	17.	T	20.	F
14.	T				

Multiple-Choice Questions

21.	c	25.	a	28.	a
22.	b	26.	a	29.	d
23.	c	27.	d	30.	b
24.	c				

Completion Questions

31. Law, society
32. U.S. Constitution
33. plaintiff, defendant
34. appellant, appellee
35. affirm, remand, reverse, dismiss
36. due process, Fifth, Fourteenth
37. treason, felonies, misdemeanors, punishment
38. contract, tort, civil
39. consideration, offer, acceptance
40. voluntarily assumed, imposed by law

CHAPTER II

Key Terms

1.	e	5.	f	8.	h
2.	k	6.	b	9.	l
3.	i	7.	j	10.	c
4.	a				

True-False Questions

11.	F	15.	T	18.	F
12.	T	16.	F	19.	T
13.	T	17.	T	20.	F
14.	T				

Multiple-Choice Questions

21.	b	25.	a	28.	c
22.	b	26.	d	29.	d
23.	a	27.	d	30.	b
24.	b				

Completion Questions

31. function, trial, appellate
32. Jurisdiction, venue
33. subject matter, *in personam, in rem*
34. district, appeals, Supreme Court
35. probate, local (municipal), small claims

CHAPTER III

Key Terms

1.	d		5.	l		8.	e	
2.	k		6.	f		9.	i	
3.	c		7.	b		10.	h	
4.	g							

True-False Questions

11.	F		15.	F		18.	F
12.	F		16.	F		19.	T
13.	T		17.	F		20.	T
14.	T						

Multiple-Choice Questions

21.	c		25.	d		28.	b
22.	b		26.	b		29.	c
23.	a		27.	c		30.	d
24.	a						

Completion Questions

31. rules, trial, litigation
32. exploratory, settlement (pretrial)
33. summons, complaint
34. complaint, answer, reply

35. dismiss, demurrer, summary, pleadings
36. discovery, oral, written, interrogatories
37. *voir dire*, cause, peremptory
38. subpoena, *subpoena duces tecum*, contempt
39. nonjury, immaterial, privilege
40. hearsay, *res gestae*
41. motion, directed, wins
42. trial, notwithstanding, relief
43. execution, lien

CHAPTER IV

Key Terms

1. h	5. i	8. d
2. c	6. e	9. l
3. j	7. k	10. f
4. b		

True-False Questions

11. T	15. F	18. T
12. T	16. F	19. F
13. F	17. F	20. T
14. T		

Multiple-Choice Questions

21. d	24. b	27. c
22. c	25. a	28. a
23. b	26. d	29. d

Completion Questions

30. case, controversy, advisory
31. Moot, ripeness, adverse
32. legislature, statute of limitations, toll
33. *res judicata*, parties, issues

34. immunity, sovereign immunity, contract
35. discretionary, proprietary, official
36. husbands, wives, parental, unemancipated

CHAPTER V

Key Terms

1.	a	5.	c	8.	b
2.	j	6.	k	9.	l
3.	i	7.	h	10.	e
4.	d				

True-False Questions

11.	T	15.	F	18.	F
12.	T	16.	T	19.	T
13.	F	17.	T	20.	F
14.	T				

Multiple-Choice Questions

21.	b	25.	a	28.	b
22.	c	26.	d	29.	c
23.	b	27.	a	30.	b
24.	c				

Completion Questions

31. *stare decisis* (precedent), binding, facts
32. majority, reported (published)
33. holding, *dicta,* precedent
34. decision, events, retroactive, prospective
35. conflict of laws, substantive, procedural
36. *lex loci delicti commissi, lex loci contractus*
37. sovereignty (entity), 4, 1, public policy
38. Comity, international

CHAPTER VI

Key Terms

1. d
2. f
3. e
4. i

5. h
6. a
7. b

8. c
9. j
10. g

True-False Questions

11. T
12. F
13. T
14. T

15. T
16. F
17. T

18. F
19. F
20. F

Multiple-Choice Questions

21. a
22. d
23. d
24. c

25. a
26. b
27. c

28. b
29. a
30. b

Completion Questions

31. equitable, common law
32. legal, money (damages), injunction
33. mandatory, prohibitory, contempt, reversed
34. permanent, preliminary, interlocutory, temporary restraining order
35. restitution, defendant's, plaintiff's
36. chancery (conscience), common law, equitable
37. conscience, precedent, equitable maxims
38. constitutional, common law, equity, jury, judge
39. compensatory, punitive, nominal, liquidated

CHAPTER VII

Key Terms

1.	b	6.	a	11.	n
2.	l	7.	m	12.	f
3.	j	8.	k	13.	h
4.	p	9.	c	14.	i
5.	e	10.	o		

True-False Questions

15.	F	20.	F	25.	F
16.	T	21.	T	26.	F
17.	F	22.	T	27.	F
18.	F	23.	F	28.	T
19.	F	24.	T	29.	F

Multiple-Choice Questions

30.	a	34.	c	38.	d
31.	b	35.	c	39.	a
32.	c	36.	c	40.	b
33.	a	37.	d		

Completion Questions

41. criminal, individuals, community
42. treason, felonies, misdemeanors, felonies
43. innocence, Fourth, Fifth, Sixth, Eighth, Fourteenth
44. incrimination, voluntarily, warnings
45. lineups, counsel
46. wrongful act, guilty mind, concurrence, causation
47. general, specific, criminal negligence, risk creation
48. warrant, probable cause
49. search, "no-knock", entering, incidental
50. liable
51. preliminary, grand jury, indictment
52. arraignment, plea, guilty, *nolo contendere*, not guilty
53. bail, recognizance

CHAPTER VIII

Key Terms

1.	b	5.	d	8.	k
2.	l	6.	f	9.	j
3.	h	7.	i	10.	e
4.	a				

True-False Questions

11.	T	15.	T	18.	T
12.	T	16.	F	19.	F
13.	F	17.	T	20.	F
14.	T				

Multiple-Choice Questions

21.	d	25.	a	28.	d
22.	c	26.	d	29.	a
23.	a	27.	b	30.	c
24.	b				

Completion Questions

31. contract, competent, assent, consideration, law
32. valid, void, voidable
33. bilateral, unilateral
34. offer, acceptance
35. duress, undue, fraud, innocent, mistake
36. Consideration, promise, act, forbearance
37. capacity, minors, insane, intoxicated
38. illegal
39. fraud, decedent, marriage, another, one year, real, goods

CHAPTER IX

Key Terms

1.	d	5.	e	8.	f
2.	g	6.	c	9.	h
3.	a	7.	b	10.	k
4.	l				

True-False Questions

11.	F	15.	T	18.	F
12.	T	16.	F	19.	F
13.	F	17.	T	20.	F
14.	F				

Multiple-Choice Questions

21.	d	25.	b	28.	a
22.	c	26.	d	29.	c
23.	b	27.	d	30.	b
24.	a				

Completion Questions

31. immovable, money, goods, movable items
32. common law, real property, Uniform Commercial Code, personalty, fixtures
33. State government, police power
34. severalty ownership, concurrent ownership, community property
35. estate in land, life estate, possessory interest, leasehold
36. license, temporary, oral, revoked at will
37. rights, obligations, mutual benefit bailment, compensation, quid pro quo
38. purchase, creation, capture, accession, finding, gift, confusion, inheritance
39. actual possession, hostile, open, notorious, statutory
40. recording system, registry of deeds, deeds, easements, options, mortgages

CHAPTER X

Key Terms

1.	d	5.	l	8.	g
2.	h	6.	c	9.	i
3.	e	7.	k	10.	j
4.	b				

True-False Questions

11.	T	15.	F	18.	T
12.	F	16.	F	19.	T
13.	T	17.	T	20.	F
14.	T				

Multiple-Choice Questions

21.	b	25.	b	28.	b
22.	d	26.	a	29.	d
23.	c	27.	b	30.	c
24.	a				

Completion Questions

31. duty, conduct, duty, injury
32. Negligence, care, reasonably, negligence, liability
33. legislative, judicial, relationship
34. invitees, licensees, trespassers, invitee
35. reasonable, proximate
36. Contributory, assumption, risk, risk
37. Imputed, agent, principal, contractor
38. intentional, intent
39. privacy, defamation
40. Libel, slander
41. Assault, battery, criminal, civil
42. conversion, contract, trespass, false
43. Strict, care, product

CHAPTER XI

Key Terms

1. e	5. h	8. k
2. j	6. b	9. f
3. a	7. i	10. g
4. l		

True-False Questions

11. T	15. F	18. T
12. T	16. F	19. F
13. T	17. T	20. T
14. F		

Multiple-Choice Questions

21. a	25. b	28. b
22. c	26. c	29. c
23. b	27. c	30. a
24. d		

Completion Questions

31. enabling, order, constitutional
32. investigation, rule making, enforcement, adjudication
33. investigate, adjudicative
34. quasi, Administrative Procedure
35. adjudicatory, judicial
36. exhaust, ripe
37. exceeded, due process, substantial

CHAPTER XII

Key Terms

1.	d	5.	j	8.	l
2.	g	6.	h	9.	k
3.	a	7.	e	10.	i
4.	b				

True-False Questions

11.	T	15.	T	18.	F
12.	T	16.	F	19.	T
13.	F	17.	F	20.	F
14.	T				

Multiple-Choice Questions

21.	d	25.	c	28.	a
22.	c	26.	a	29.	b
23.	d	27.	d	30.	c
24.	b				

Completion Questions

31. court, a jury trial
32. pregnancy, Pregnancy Discrimination Act
33. intent, disparate impact discrimination
34. employee, persuading, pretext
35. racial discrimination, initially hired, discriminatory treatment
36. 25 or more, 15 or more
37. remedy, previous record, consent agreements or decrees
38. union, associate with, bargain collectively
39. union elections, certifies, hears and settles, unfair labor practices
40. race, religion, sex, racial origin

CHAPTER XIII

Key Terms

1.	h	5.	b	8.	c
2.	k	6.	d	9.	l
3.	g	7.	j	10.	f
4.	a				

True-False Questions

11.	F	15.	F	18.	T
12.	F	16.	T	19.	F
13.	T	17.	T	20.	F
14.	T				

Multiple-Choice Questions

21.	b	24.	c	27.	a
22.	d	25.	a	28.	a
23.	d	26.	b		

Completion Questions

29. Sherman Act, Clayton Act, Federal Trade Commission Act
30. preserve, promote, interstate commerce
31. Clayton Act
32. interlocking directorates, competing, potentially could
33. product, geographic, price, competition
34. Sherman Act, fine, imprisonment, injunction, punitive, seize
35. price differential, actual cost savings, quantity, marketability, good faith
36. rule of reason, unreasonably restrain
37. civil and criminal, federal
38. tying, purchases, product, service, illegal per se

CHAPTER XIV

Key Terms

1.	h	5.	g	8.	e
2.	f	6.	k	9.	l
3.	b	7.	a	10.	j
4.	i				

True-False Questions

11.	F	15.	F	18.	T
12.	F	16.	T	19.	T
13.	T	17.	F	20.	F
14.	T				

Multiple-Choice Questions

21.	d	24.	d	27.	c
22.	c	25.	c	28.	a
23.	b	26.	b		

Completion Questions

29. mandatory, nonbinding
30. mediation, mini-trials, judicially hosted settlement conferences, summary jury trials, arbitrations, private trials
31. reject, penalty, substantial fine
32. identify what they want, narrows, alternatives, options, focusing only on one solution
33. precedent, written explanations for their award
34. findings of fact